FRANKLIN D. ROOSEVELT

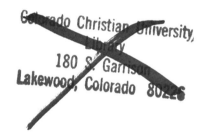

FRANKLIN D. ROOSEVELT

BRYAN J. GRAPES, *Book Editor*

DAVID L. BENDER, *Publisher*
BRUNO LEONE, *Executive Editor*
BONNIE SZUMSKI, *Editorial Director*
STUART B. MILLER, *Managing Editor*
JAMES D. TORR, *Series Editor*

GREENHAVEN PRESS, INC.
SAN DIEGO, CALIFORNIA

Library of Congress Cataloging-in-Publication Data

Franklin D. Roosevelt / Bryan J. Grapes, book editor.
        p.   cm. — (Presidents and their decisions)
    Includes bibliographical references (p.   ) and index.
    ISBN 0-7377-0503-5 (pbk. : alk. paper) — ISBN 0-7377-0504-3
(lib. : alk. paper)
    1. Roosevelt, Franklin D. (Franklin Delano), 1882–1945. 2. United
States—Politics and government—1933–1945—Decision making.
I. Grapes, Bryan J. II. Series.

E806 .F6914 2001
973.917'092—dc21   00-024497
                                                                CIP

Cover photo: Bettmann/Corbis
Archives of the Simon Wiesenthal Center, 197
FDR Library, 16, 170
Library of Congress, 18, 19, 25, 26, 29, 38, 57, 75, 130
National Archives, 23, 43, 181, 189

Series Design: LiMiTeD Edition Book Design, Linda Mae Tratechaud

©2001 Greenhaven Press, Inc.
P.O. Box 289009, San Diego, CA 92198-9009

PRINTED IN THE U.S.A.

Contents

Chapter One: The New Deal

CHAPTER TWO: THE COURT PACKING PLAN

CHAPTER THREE: AMERICAN INTERVENTION IN WORLD WAR II

Chapter Four: Roosevelt's Treatment of Minorities

FOREWORD

"THE PRESIDENCY OF THE UNITED STATES IS OFTEN DE-scribed as the most powerful office in the world," writes Forrest McDonald in *The American Presidency: An Intellectual History.* "In one sense this description is accurate," he says, "for even casual decisions made in the White House can affect the lives of millions of people." But Mc-Donald also notes that presidential power "is restrained by the countervailing power of Congress, the courts, the bureaucracy, popular opinion, the news media, and state and local governments. What presidents do have is awesome responsibilities combined with unique opportunities to persuade others to do their bidding—opportunities enhanced by the possibility of dispensing favors, by the mystique of presidential power, and by the aura of monarchy that surrounds the president."

The way various presidents have used the complex power of their office is the subject of Greenhaven Press's Presidents and Their Decisions series. Each volume in the series examines one particular president and the key decisions he made while in office.

Some presidential decisions have been made in a relatively brief period of time, as with Abraham Lincoln's suspension of the writ of habeus corpus at the start of the Civil War. Others were refined as they were implemented over a period of years, as was the case with Franklin Delano Roosevelt's struggle to lead the country out of the Great Depression. Some presidential actions are generally lauded by historians—for example, Lyndon Johnson's support of the civil rights movement in the 1960s—while others have been condemned—such as Richard Nixon's efforts, from 1972 to 1974, to cover up the involvement of his aides in the Watergate scandal.

Most of the truly history-making presidential decisions, though, remain the subject of intense scrutiny and historical debate. Many of these were made during a time of war or other crisis, in which a president was forced to risk either spectacular success or devastating failure. Examples include Lincoln's much-scrutinized handling of the crisis at Fort Sumter, the first conflict of the Civil War; FDR's efforts to aid the European Allies at the beginning of World War II; Harry Truman's controversial decision to use the atomic bomb in order to end that conflict; and Lyndon Johnson's fateful decision to escalate the war in Vietnam.

Each volume in the Presidents and Their Decisions series devotes a full chapter to each of the president's key decisions. The essays in each chapter, most written by presidential historians and biographers, offer a range of perspectives on the president and his actions. Some provide background on the political, social, and economic factors behind a particular decision. Others critique the president's performance, offering a negative or positive appraisal. Essays have been chosen for their concise and engaging presentation of the facts, and each is preceded by a straightforward summary of the article's content.

In addition to the articles, these books include extensive material to help the student researcher. An opening essay provides both a brief biography of the president and an overview of the events that occurred during his time in office. A chronology also helps readers keep track of the dates of specific events. A comprehensive index and an annotated table of contents aid readers in quickly locating material of interest, and an extensive bibliography serves as a launching point for further research. Finally, an appendix of primary historical documents provides a sampling of the president's most important speeches, as well as some of his contemporaries' criticisms.

Greenhaven Press's Presidents and Their Decisions series will help students gain a deeper understanding of the decisions made by some of the most influential leaders in American history.

FRANKLIN DELANO ROOSEVELT: A BIOGRAPHY

INAUGURATION DAY ON MARCH 4, 1933, DAWNED COLD AND rainy—a fitting reflection of the somber mood of America. On this inhospitable day, Franklin Delano Roosevelt was sworn in as the thirty-second president of a nation in the grip of its worst crisis since the Civil War. A destructive financial chain reaction, set in motion by the stock market crash of October 1929, created a severe economic depression that affected not only the United States but most of the industrialized world as well. As banks failed and unemployment spiraled ever-upward, Franklin Delano Roosevelt, promising a "New Deal" to Americans suffering the calamitous effects of the economic disaster, assumed the presidency of a nation that many felt was on the verge of collapse. In what is thought to be one of the most stirring speeches in American history, Roosevelt rallied a stricken nation to action:

> I am certain that my fellow-Americans expect that on my induction to the Presidency I will address them with a candor and a decision which the present situation of our Nation impels. This is pre-eminently the time to speak the truth, the whole truth, frankly and boldly. Nor need we shrink from honestly facing conditions in our country today. This great Nation will endure as it has endured, will revive and prosper. So first of all let me assert my firm belief that the only thing we have to fear is fear itself—nameless, unreasoning, unjustified terror which paralyzes needed efforts to convert retreat into advance. In every dark hour of our national life a leadership of frankness and vigor has met with that understanding and support of the people themselves which is essential to victory. I am convinced that you will again give that support to leadership in these critical days.[1]

With these words, Roosevelt confidently took his place in the White House. Not only did he hold the office of president longer than any other person in American history, Roosevelt drastically redefined the nature of the presidency while guiding the United States through two of the worst crises of the twentieth century—the Great Depression and World War II.

The Early Years

According to biographer Nathan Miller, "Probably no President of the United States had a happier and more secure childhood than Franklin Roosevelt."[2] Franklin was born into a life of wealth and privilege in Hyde Park, New York, on January 30, 1882. He was the only child born to his parents, Sara Delano, a doting and sometimes overbearing mother who could trace her ancestry back to the *Mayflower*, and James Roosevelt, a widower twenty-six years her senior, whose great-grandfather took part in New York's ratification of the Constitution. Without brothers or sisters (James did have an adult son from his previous marriage) to compete for his parents' affection, Franklin was showered with attention. Though he was socially sheltered and raised in the manner of a country squire, Franklin's parents took great care to instill in him a charitable nature and a sense of social responsibility. Sara once wrote her son that "nothing is so helpful to ourselves as doing for others and trying to sink all selfishness."[3]

Private tutors administered Franklin Roosevelt's early education so that he could accompany his parents on their frequent travels. When he reached the age of fourteen, he was sent to Groton, an exclusive boarding school in Massachusetts thirty-five miles north of Boston. Under the tutelage of the academy's headmaster, Reverend Endicott Peabody, Franklin's sense of social responsibility was reinforced, and throughout his years at Groton Roosevelt was active in religious and charitable work.

For the first time in his life, Franklin was outside of the protective world his parents provided at the family estate in Hyde Park, and among a crowd of boys his own age. Though he was a good student, Franklin had a difficult time fitting in with the other boys at Groton. He excelled on the debating team, but was a less-than-gifted athlete (and athletics were the one surefire path to acceptance among the Groton students). As graduation neared, Franklin expressed an interest in attending the United States Naval Academy, but his parents would not allow it. Instead, he enrolled in Groton's "anticipation" plan for Harvard, which would allow Roosevelt to complete the requirements for a bachelor's degree in three years instead of four.

Life at Harvard

Roosevelt entered Harvard in the fall of 1900. Determined to remedy his awkward social standing at Groton, Franklin engaged in a wide range of social, athletic, political, and extracurricular activities while at Harvard. The most notable of his achievements during this time was his election to the highly coveted position of president, or editor-in-chief, of the *Crimson*, Harvard's newspaper. Though athletics continued to be a source of frustration for him at Harvard, Roosevelt pursued them with enthusiasm, playing on one of the intramural football teams after being cut from the freshman squad. Roosevelt's political life began at the university when he joined the Harvard Republican Club, despite the Democratic leanings of his family. Though he was still too young to vote, he enthusiastically pitched in for distant cousin Theodore Roosevelt's campaign for the vice presidency in 1900. As at Groton, Roosevelt continued to be active with a number of charitable organizations and was involved with a number of causes for the less fortunate.

For all his attempts at fitting in, however, Roosevelt was not widely accepted at Harvard. He was perceived by many to be a frivolous snob and he suffered his first social rejection at Harvard—being passed over for entrance into the exclusive Delta Kappa Epsilon fraternity. Roosevelt's confidence and breezy manner irked many of his peers, as it was sometimes interpreted as arrogance. Some of his classmates regarded him as too aggressive and too eager to be liked, which made him appear insincere at times. According to Eleanor Roosevelt, Franklin's future wife, his schoolmates at Groton and Harvard "didn't like him. They had to give him a certain recognition because of his intellectual ability. But he was never of the inner clique."[4] This inability to fit in would remain with Roosevelt throughout his life and many of Roosevelt's contemporaries attributed it to his lack of experience with people his own age. As Mike Reilly, a Secret Service agent who saw Roosevelt on a daily basis in the White House, put it, he always wanted to be "one of the boys. He was never 'one of the boys' although he frequently made a good try," Reilly observed. "It was such a good try that it never quite came off."[5]

Marriage

Roosevelt completed the requirements for his degree in the spring of 1903, but he remained at Harvard for an additional year to finish his term at the *Crimson*. Earlier in the year, Roosevelt had met and begun to court his distant cousin Eleanor. Eleanor was niece to Theodore Roosevelt (who became president after the assassination of William McKinley in 1901), whose career Franklin hoped to emulate. She accepted his proposal of marriage and they were wed on March 17, 1905, in a ceremony performed by Endicott Peabody and in which President Theodore Roosevelt gave the bride away. The marriage produced six children: Anna, born in 1906; James, born in 1907; Franklin Jr., born in 1909 and died in infancy; Elliott, born in 1910; a second Franklin Jr., born in 1914; and John, born in 1916.

Just before his marriage to Eleanor, Roosevelt enrolled

in Columbia Law School in New York City. He found law school to be dull and was restless at Columbia. Roosevelt passed the bar examination in the spring of 1907 and did not bother to return to Columbia to finish his law degree.

FDR married his distant cousin, Eleanor, on March 17, 1905. Six children resulted from the union: Anna, James, Franklin Jr., Elliot, a second Franklin Jr. (the first died in infancy), and John.

Life as a lawyer was not a fulfilling experience for him. His associates thought him a bright and competent attorney, but Roosevelt felt unchallenged and he remarked to his colleagues that he did not wish to practice law forever. For some time Roosevelt had planned on following his cousin Theodore's example by going into politics. He felt that he had a real chance to be president one day, and the course that Franklin Roosevelt plotted to the White House duplicated the one followed by his cousin Theodore: First, he would win a seat in the New York state legislature, secure an appointment as assistant secretary of the Navy, be elected governor of New York, and finally, enter the Oval Office.

The Road to the Presidency

Most of the Roosevelt family, particularly Franklin's mother, tried to persuade him to keep out of the political world. In their estimation, a political career was not suitable for a man of Franklin's breeding. Roosevelt ignored his family's advice and in 1910 he was nominated as the Democratic candidate for state senator from New York's twenty-sixth district. A Roosevelt victory was considered by many to be impossible, as he was running against a firmly entrenched incumbent in a heavily Republican district. Campaigning tirelessly, Roosevelt scored an upset victory over Republican John F. Schlosser.

The upset victory brought Roosevelt to the attention of many important leaders in the Democratic Party, among them New Jersey governor Woodrow Wilson, with whom he shared a progressive vision of government. Among the reforms both supported was the direct election of U.S. senators (who at that time were selected by the state legislatures), regulation of business abuses, and conservation of natural resources. In addition to Theodore Roosevelt, Woodrow Wilson was to become one of Franklin Roosevelt's most influential role models, and Franklin Roosevelt became one of Woodrow Wilson's most ardent sup-

Despite his family's discouragement, Roosevelt entered politics by running for state senator of New York's twenty-sixth district in 1910. His upset win brought him to the attention of many important Democrats; including future president Woodrow Wilson (pictured).

porters. Roosevelt was one of the leaders in the campaign to get Wilson the Democratic Party's presidential nomination in 1912. Wilson went on to win the election, and in March 1913 he appointed Franklin Roosevelt assistant secretary of the Navy, a post he occupied for seven years.

World War I

As assistant secretary of the Navy, Roosevelt had a close view of national and world events that foreshadowed circumstances he was to face during his own presidency. The assassination of Austrian archduke Franz Ferdinand in Sarajevo in June 1914 triggered a wave of war declarations in Europe. By the end of that year massive armies waged an unprecedented level of warfare across the whole continent.

Holding the post for seven years, FDR became concerned about international affairs while serving as President Wilson's assistant secretary of the Navy.

Roosevelt was one of the few in American government who felt that the United States would not be able to remain completely isolated from the events in Europe. The isolationist sentiments of the American public and the government frustrated Roosevelt. He felt that the military should be gathered into a high state of readiness, just in case the United States was drawn into the war. In a letter to Eleanor, Roosevelt complained that many in Wilson's cabinet completely failed to "grasp the fact that this war between the other powers is going inevitably to give rise to a hundred different complications in which we shall have a direct interest. Questions of refugees, of neutrality, of commerce are even now appearing and we should unquestionably gather our fleet together and get it into the highest state of efficiency."[6]

President Wilson, meanwhile, resisted efforts toward military preparedness. The president, desperate to keep the United States neutral and mindful of the American public's reluctance to become embroiled in European affairs, worried that any mobilization of armed forces—even those wholly defensive in nature— would be interpreted as an act of war. By 1917, however, the German military's policy of unrestricted submarine warfare—a policy that claimed the lives of many American civilians—forced Wilson to ask Congress for a declaration of war against Germany.

In addition to marking the first time the United States would be exercising direct military influence in the affairs of Europe, the American declaration of war began a massive concentration of power in the hands of the federal government. The government assumed direct control of the production and consumption of food and fuel, shipbuilding, and foreign trade—a kind of state-controlled capitalism that the New Deal would later emulate. In preparing America for war, President Wilson had to fight long-entrenched feelings of isolationism in Congress and the public—a similar dilemma that the future President

Roosevelt would have to face when war clouds darkened over Europe again in the 1930s.

As assistant secretary of the Navy, Roosevelt acquired a skill for the politics of administration. His duties included the handling of labor relations: He was responsible for overseeing jobs involving close to 100,000 civilian employees and he personally participated in wage hearings and negotiations with labor leaders. By the end of the Wilson years, Roosevelt had acquired a reputation for being a strong friend of organized labor.

In addition to highlighting his skills as a hands-on leader, Roosevelt's time in the Navy department also brought to light some of the darker aspects of his personality. He was regularly insubordinate and critical of his superiors, Navy secretary Josephus Daniels and President Wilson. Roosevelt was not known as a team player. Some historians believe that this merely indicated that Roosevelt's skills and temperament made him better suited to lead as opposed to working with a group. But others saw him as overly ambitious and self-serving. He was impatient and quick to take credit for the successes of the Navy, and just as quick to pass out blame for failures. Many interpreted his enthusiasm to get the job done as a personal thirst for power. Referring to similar problems he had witnessed with Franklin's cousin Theodore, Senator Elihu Root noted to Daniels upon Roosevelt's appointment as his assistant, "Whenever a Roosevelt rides, he wishes to ride in front."[7]

Roosevelt Is Stricken by Polio

Following his term as assistant secretary of the Navy, Roosevelt made a failed bid for the vice presidency as the running mate of James M. Cox in the election of 1920. After that he returned to life as a lawyer. On the morning of August 11, 1921, during the first uninterrupted summer vacation with his family since his appointment to the Navy department, Roosevelt swung out of bed and discovered that his left leg lagged. His right leg soon collapsed and he dragged himself back to bed with a fever of 102 degrees. The next day he could not move his legs at all. Roosevelt was soon diagnosed with poliomyelitis, a crippling disease for which there was no cure. He was paralyzed from the waist down and would never again be able to walk unaided. For Roosevelt, an active man in the prime of his life who enjoyed the outdoors and physical activity, it was a devastating blow. Not only did polio put an end to the active lifestyle that he enjoyed, but the disease also spelled what nearly everyone believed to be certain doom for Roosevelt's political career. At that time, no one thought that a paralyzed man would be able to win high political office. The disease, however, was to have a very different effect on his career and his personality.

It is generally acknowledged, by Roosevelt's contemporaries and historians alike, that Roosevelt's battle with polio marked a striking turning point in his personal and political development. Though he had been steeped in the philosophy of social responsibility since childhood, his feelings toward charity and social justice were often interpreted as an insincere, "be good to the peasants" attitude. Though a capable politician and leader, his early career was marred by incidents of insubordination, impatience, and arrogance. More than a few observers felt that Roosevelt's battle with polio eradicated these negative aspects of his personality. Frances Perkins, who served as secretary of labor during Roosevelt's terms as governor of New York and president, believed that his battle with paralysis not only allowed Roosevelt to mature and outgrow his emotional shortcomings, but that his suffering made him the ideal man to lead the nation from the misery and economic paralysis of the Great Depression. According to Perkins,

> Franklin Roosevelt underwent a spiritual transformation during the years of his illness. I noticed that when

Frances Perkins, FDR's secretary of labor, believed that his battle with paralysis made him a more effective leader.

he came back that the years of pain and suffering had purged the slightly arrogant attitude he had displayed on occasion before he was stricken. He emerged completely warmhearted, with humility of spirit and with deeper philosophy. Having been to the depths of trouble, he understood the problems of people in trouble.[8]

Governor Roosevelt

Following his years of rehabilitation at Warm Springs (a spa in Georgia), Roosevelt returned to the national political stage as an instrumental figure in the nomination of New York governor Al Smith as the Democratic candidate for president in the election of 1928. In return, Smith lent his support to Roosevelt's campaign to succeed him as governor. Responding to the mounting questions in the press about Roosevelt's physical health, Smith remarked: "A governor does not have to be an acrobat. We do not elect him for his ability to do a double back-flip or a handspring. The work of the Governorship is brainwork. Ninety-nine per cent of it is accomplished behind a desk."[9] With the question of his physical health behind him, Roosevelt won the election, despite a nationwide Republican sweep.

The beginning of Roosevelt's tenure as New York's governor was rather uneventful. The nation was riding a wave of unprecedented prosperity and Roosevelt's most substantial contributions to New York were minor progressive reforms he instituted in the prison, legal, and banking systems. In addition to these, Roosevelt established himself as a leading proponent of agricultural reforms to alleviate the burden felt by New York's farmers who, even in this pre-depression era of prosperity, were feeling the pressure from steadily falling produce prices. He also established himself as a prominent supporter of the development of cheap electrical power and persuaded the legislature to create a state power authority—a prophetic glimpse of the creation of the Tennessee Valley Authority—and continued to build his reputation as a friend of organized labor.

During the years he was governor, Roosevelt began to make use of a relatively new medium to drum up popular support for his policies—the radio. He gave regular addresses to the citizens of New York. His speeches were simple, straightforward, and friendly in tone, and they were the forerunners of Roosevelt's famous "fireside chats." Despite his progressive agenda, Roosevelt's first year as governor secured him a reputation as a rather conservative politician. This changed when the stock market crashed, and the United States started a long downward spiral into despair.

The Great Depression

Though other factors contributed to the economic calamity that became know as the Great Depression, it is generally acknowledged that the stock market crash of October 1929 was the event that sparked the destructive financial chain reaction. America had endured cycles of boom and bust before, but never had the economy taken such a dramatic and widespread downturn. While President Herbert Hoover optimistically predicted a speedy recovery, the nation sank to new economic lows. Unemployment, which had hovered at about 3 percent before the crash, rose to 9 percent in 1930. By 1933 the unemployment rate had risen to a catastrophic 25 percent—17 million people in all. The unemployment rate for African Americans was closer to 50 percent. National income fell to half of what it had been before October 1929. Farm prices were practically nonexistent, having dropped 60 percent from the already depressed levels of 1929. Farmers all over the country were losing their farms to foreclosure. Share values on Wall Street, which had skyrocketed to $87 billion before the crash, plummeted to $19 billion. To make matters worse, many investors had purchased their stocks on margin. This meant that a bank loaned the investor the money to buy stock, which in turn served as the collateral for the loan. Since the stock was close to worthless after the crash, borrowers could not pay off their loans and banks could not collect. Once depositors started to withdraw their funds the banks became insolvent and collapsed, wiping out the savings of many depositors.

At first, the number of bank failures was small and widely dispersed. This prevented the banking problem from reaching crisis proportions for the first year of the depression. By 1933, however, close to 10,000 banks had failed. Of the bank failures that occurred during the depression, the most disastrous was that of the prestigious and once powerful Bank of the United States. When the Bank of the United States closed its doors, 450,000 depositors were left wondering what would become of their life savings.

Roosevelt Changes His Approach

President Hoover and the Republican leadership held to the traditional American notion of laissez-faire—or hands off—government, which held that business was able to regulate it-

Herbert Hoover

self and that government involvement was bad for profits. What was good for business was good for the country. The depression was initially viewed as a natural downswing of the economic cycle that would eventually correct itself. Hoover did try to stimulate the economy in limited ways, however. The Reconstruction Finance Corporation (RFC) was set up to lend money to businesses in the hopes that it would create jobs and stimulate spending. A limited public works program was set up to create even more jobs and provide the nation with highways, schools, and dams, but that was as far as the Hoover administration was willing to go to cure the nation's ills. Hoover felt that relief measures were better left to the states and private charities. In his view, federal involvement with relief measures would erode the American spirit of self-help and make the public perpetually reliant upon government charity.

During the first years of the depression Roosevelt felt much the same way as Hoover about business regulation and relief measures. Roosevelt had even condemned the Hoover administration's conservative attempts to stimulate the economy as too radical and costly. The failure of the Bank of the United States, however, marked a reverse in Roosevelt's philosophy. When the bank was teetering on the verge of collapse, Roosevelt invited some of the biggest bankers and businessmen in New York to his home to negotiate a merger that would save it from failing. He was struck by the nonchalant attitude of these businessmen. They felt that if the bank were going to fail, they should let it fail. It was then that Roosevelt came to believe that business was incapable of regulating itself, and that the depression was not a natural part of the economic cycle, but a result of wild, unchecked speculation on the stock market and unscrupulous business practices. As he watched the misery of the depression mount, he became convinced that government should serve as more than just caretaker to a prosperous economy—government had an obligation to ensure the well-being of its citizens. "What is the State?" Roosevelt asked in a message to the state legislature. "It is the duly constituted representation of an organized society of human beings, created by them for their mutual protection and well-being. 'The State' or 'the Government' is but the machinery through which such mutual aid and protection are achieved. . . . I assert that modern society, acting through its government, owes the definite obligation to prevent the starvation or dire want of any of its fellow men and women who try to maintain themselves but cannot."[10]

Although Roosevelt has been blamed for creating an inefficient welfare system in the U.S., he believed that the government has a responsibility to protect its citizens from starvation and poverty.

Roosevelt introduced sweeping action in New York to combat the depression. He authorized the use of National Guard armories to house the homeless and he set up a commission to study the feasibility of unemployment insurance. He proposed an eight-hour workday and a five-day workweek to prevent workers from being laid off (at the time the average workday was twelve hours and the average workweek six days). Roosevelt's Temporary Emergency Relief Administration (TERA) distributed $25 million to the needy, half of which was spent to create jobs in the form of public works projects. This blaze of activity marked a striking departure from that of President Hoover. Roosevelt's actions made him the frontrunner in his party's race for the presidential nomination. After securing the Democratic nomination, Roosevelt went on to trounce Herbert Hoover in the election of 1932.

President Roosevelt

Roosevelt's most pressing task after his inauguration was to stem the bank crisis. On March 6, 1933, two days after he had assumed office, he summoned a special session of Congress and delivered his proposal for a national "bank holiday." Roosevelt recommended that all banks in the country close down and show their books to the federal government. The government would then extend emergency aid to those banks that needed it, and only those whose finances were sound would be allowed to reopen. The House of Representatives passed the bill without even taking the time to read it in its entirety. The Senate quickly followed suit and Roosevelt's bank bill reached his desk for his signature seven hours after he submitted it to Congress. It was the fastest passage of a bill in U.S. history. Roosevelt then addressed the nation in the first of many "fireside chats." In the address Roosevelt assured the public of the safety of their deposits and urged them to not withdraw all of their money when the banks reopened. When the banks reopened they report-

In an attempt to restore the public's confidence in the U.S. economy and encourage investments, FDR signed a bill in March of 1933 designed to reform the U.S. banking system.

ed that for the first time in years, deposits outnumbered withdrawals. The banking crisis was over.

The unprecedented swell of support from the public and Congress allowed Roosevelt—aided by a group of advisers known as the "Brain Trust"—to enact an avalanche of legislation in the first three months of his presidency, which became known as the Hundred Days. To remedy the plight of the nation's farmers, he introduced the Agricultural Adjustment Act (AAA). Roosevelt theorized that the dramatically low farm prices plaguing the agricultural system were the result of overproduction. The AAA was designed to increase the profits of farmers by having them reduce production of wheat, corn, rice, and other crops. To tackle the unemployment problem, Roosevelt created the Civilian Conservation Corps (CCC), and the Public Works Administration (PWA). The CCC put some 2.7 million people to work in the nation's forests planting trees, fighting forest fires, and building dams. The PWA contracted with private companies to build schools, hospitals, roads, bridges, and sewage systems, providing half a million jobs a year to those who desperately needed work. The president created the Tennessee Valley Authority (TVA) to develop electrical power in the Tennessee River Valley. The huge dams that were built by the TVA provided millions of Americans with cheap electricity and created years of work for thousands of people. The National Industrial Recovery Act (NIRA) was designed to regulate and stimulate business and set the nation's economy back on its feet. The Securities Act created the Securities and Exchange Commission (SEC), which was to police Wall Street and prevent the wild speculation that led to the crash.

Perhaps the most far-reaching program of Roosevelt's presidency was the Social Security Act. Signed into law on August 14, 1935, the Social Security Act, which affects wage earners and retirees to this day, provided aid for citizens who were in need because of increasing age, unemployment, or sickness. Contributions from employers and wage earners go into a fund that distributes the money to people over the age of 65, temporarily out of a job, or otherwise unable to work. The Social Security Act, along with the other programs that became collectively known as the New Deal, were intended to insure against future depressions. Roosevelt knew that he could not guarantee endless prosperity, but he want to make sure that the misery of the early 1930s was never repeated.

When Congress adjourned exactly one hundred days after the special session opened, it had approved the most extraordinary set of reforms in American history. The reform measures of the New Deal remade the face of American government in such dramatic fashion that it became known as the "Roosevelt Revolution." The New Deal involved the government in business and the lives of its citizens to an unprecedented extent, but the effect it had on the depression became a source of debate.

Historical Evaluation of the New Deal

Noted journalist and Roosevelt critic John T. Flynn contends that Roosevelt's policies did little more than raise government spending and increase the national debt to record levels. Despite the eight years of unrivaled federal spending during Roosevelt's first two terms, Flynn asserts, the nation was no closer to breaking the grip of the depression than it had been when Roosevelt first assumed office.

> In his first two full terms of eight years, President Roosevelt never produced any recovery whatever. When he was elected there were 11,586,000 persons unemployed. In 1939—seven years later—when the war struck in Europe, there were still 11,369,000 persons unemployed. . . . In 1932 when he was elected there were 4,155,000 households with 16,620,000 persons on relief. In 1939, seven years later, there were 4,227,000 households with 19,648,000 persons on relief. In the presence of these undisputed facts how can any sober-minded citizen suppose that Mr. Roosevelt brought recovery to the United States?[11]

Only when the defense industry was mobilized to provide massive amounts of machinery and arms for World War II did the United States finally pull itself out of the depression, Flynn argues.

Historian Samuel Eliot Morison, however, argues that in spite of its flaws, the New Deal was a success because "it gave the ordinary citizen a feeling of financial security against old age, sickness, and unemployment which he had never enjoyed, and a participation in government such as he had never felt since Lincoln's era." Moreover, Morison asserts, laissez-faire government led directly to the rise of fascism in Europe. Because the German and Italian governments made no effort to alleviate the misery that the Great Depression wreaked upon their citizens, men like Hitler and Mussolini were able to seize power. Morison contends that the same may have happened in the United States were it not for President Roosevelt. "There is no knowing what might have happened under another administration like Hoover's," Morison argues. "The German Republic fell before Hitler largely because it kept telling the people, 'The government can do nothing for you.'"[12] By purging the capitalist system of its worst excesses, President Roosevelt saved the American system of government, Morison contends.

The New Deal and African Americans

Some historians criticize the New Deal because its relief efforts were at times highly selective. African Americans had been especially hard hit by the depression. Whereas unemployment for whites had hit 25 percent, unemployment for African Americans averaged about 50 percent, and in some rural southern towns as many as 90 percent of African Americans were on some kind of relief. In addition to economic hard times, African Americans had to cope with racism and segregation, especially in the southern states (Jim Crow laws were still decades away from being eradicated by the Supreme Court). Segregation and discriminatory practices filtered down through most of the New Deal's relief efforts as well. African Americans laboring on public works projects received less pay than whites—if they were hired at all—and in many southern states white politicians made it more difficult for African Americans to obtain relief. During the first year of his presidency Roosevelt was silent on the subject of discrimination. By the close of his first term, however, the dire situation of African Americans slowly began to change.

In May 1935 President Roosevelt signed Executive Order 7046, abolishing discriminatory practices in the WPA. In March of 1937, President Roosevelt appointed the first black federal judge in American history, William Hastie. In all, Roosevelt appointed over one hundred

African Americans to federal posts. Although it was generally perceived to be half-hearted, the president eventually lent his support to anti-lynching and anti-poll tax legislation. In 1941 Roosevelt signed Executive Order 8802, creating the Committee on Fair Employment Practice. The order also banned discrimination in the defense industry. African Americans also found that they had a staunch ally in First Lady Eleanor Roosevelt. Mrs. Roosevelt worked tirelessly to end discrimination and segregation and, to the dismay of many southern politicians, was often able to influence her husband on such matters.

Though Roosevelt started to make an effort to end some discriminatory practices, he was often criticized for offering the weakest possible version of anti-discriminatory measures. According to many historians, Roosevelt was fearful of offending powerful southern Democratic politicians in Congress, who were major supporters of the president's New Deal and staunch supporters of Jim Crow laws. Historian Harvard Sitkoff writes:

> Hard times set the contours of New Deal policy. . . . The electorate wanted relief and recovery. All else had to wait. . . ."First things come first," the president emphasized repeatedly, "and I can't alienate certain votes I need for measures that would entail a fight."[13]

President Roosevelt would remain mindful of the sway of southern Democrats whenever racial issues surfaced.

The Supreme Court Steps In

Though he had his share of critics, for the first few years of Roosevelt's presidency his programs were passed practically unopposed. Roosevelt had the benefit of the most cooperative Congress of all time, as well as the overwhelming support of the public. Roosevelt asked for and was granted broad executive power to combat the depression. He practically dictated to Congress what he wanted, and they acquiesced. In 1936, after winning reelection in the most lopsided vote in American history, he was the most powerful president to ever occupy the executive office. The only threat to New Deal legislation came from the Supreme Court.

The Supreme Court's invalidation of the NIRA in 1935 marked the first serious challenge for Roosevelt and his reforms. By invalidating the NIRA, the Supreme Court, dominated by a bloc of conservative justices, ruled that Roosevelt had overstepped the constitutional bounds of his office. It was the first in a series of battles between the president and the tribunal. The Court later ruled that the AAA was unconstitutional and it invalidated a New York state minimum wage law as well. Many Roosevelt supporters worried that the Social Security Act would be next.

In February 1937, with the Court threatening to undo all of his reforms, Roosevelt submitted to Congress a plan to liberalize the Court by adding six justices to the bench. He offered what many felt was a less than valid excuse for altering the number of justices: the advanced age of the justices was contributing to rising inefficiency in handling the caseload. Therefore, the president proposed appointing an additional judge for each one that refused to retire at the age of seventy, with the number of new appointees not to exceed six. Opponents of the plan, among whom numbered many of Roosevelt's most enthusiastic supporters, did not put much stock in the president's argument. Most saw the scheme as an attempt to pack the Court with justices that would be more supportive of Roosevelt's reforms. Moreover, though many in Congress did not object to altering the size of the Supreme Court, they did object to the tactics that Roosevelt employed to try to get his plan approved. Roosevelt planned his court proposal in secrecy and submitted it to Congress without consulting key senators and congressmen. It appeared that the president was telling Congress what should be done with the Court instead of consulting with them on possible solutions. In addition to the reservations of key congressmen and senators, a stunning reversal in Supreme Court rulings on New Deal legislation seemed to make judicial reorganization unlikely and unnecessary. While debate on the plan raged, the Supreme Court issued favorable rulings on the Social Security Act and a Washington state minimum wage law that was practically identical to the New York law the Court had invalidated earlier. It appeared that President Roosevelt got what he wanted—Supreme Court approval of the New Deal. The president's desire for passage of his court proposal, however, remained undiminished.

Though his aim of liberalizing the Court had ultimately been realized, historians almost universally perceive the president's stubborn persistence in the court plan as a monumental mistake. By refusing to back down, Roosevelt himself orchestrated his spectacular defeat by the hand of Congress—a Congress that had been uncommonly cooperative until the court proposal. In addition to losing Republican support for any further New Deal legislation, Roosevelt opened an enormous rift in his own Democratic Party and exposed himself to the possibility of future defeat. According to Kenneth S. Davis, Roosevelt's "sadly mistaken court-packing effort effectively ended the New Deal as a reforming, transforming social force."[14]

War Clouds Over Europe

While the president was locked in battle with the Supreme Court, events in Europe threatened to plunge that continent into war for the second time in twenty years. Chancellor Adolf Hitler of Germany was openly flouting the terms of the Treaty of Versailles. He rearmed Germany in spectacular fashion and began to reclaim territories that had been taken from Germany at the close of the First World War. European leaders at first tried a policy of appeasement, with the hopes that Hitler would be satisfied with reclaiming lost German territory. These hopes were dashed on the morning of September 1, 1939, when Hitler sent waves of Nazi troops into neighboring Poland. Making good on their promise to defend Poland against Nazi aggression, France and Great Britain declared war on Germany.

President Roosevelt responded to the events in Europe by immediately issuing a proclamation of American neutrality. Though Roosevelt was deeply critical of Nazi policies, he was mindful of the American public's reluctance to get involved in another European war. Most had come to believe that U.S. involvement in the First World War had been a tragic mistake. Thousands of Americans had perished on European battlefields to make the world safe for democracy and to eradicate the possibility of future wars, and yet, less than twenty years later, war erupted across the continent once more. While sympathetic to France and Great Britain, many Americans were determined not to repeat the folly of intervention. Numerous opinion polls at this time indicated that an overwhelming majority of Americans were against direct intervention in the conflict.

By 1940, the Allied prospects for survival had darkened considerably. By June, Nazi troops were in Paris and England was preparing for an imminent invasion. From August until October, the Battle of Britain raged in the skies over England. Germany's objective was to destroy the Royal Air Force (RAF) and secure the skies over the English Channel for the invasion. In the early days of the battle the Luftwaffe (Germany's air force) came perilously close to destroying the RAF and some Americans wondered with President Roosevelt about America's place in a Nazi-dominated world. If England fell to the Nazis, there would be no barrier between the U.S. and a Nazi-dominated Europe but the Atlantic Ocean. America would be exposed to a very real threat of invasion. While formally remaining out of the conflict, Roosevelt took increasingly bold steps to provide desperately needed material assistance to England.

The Lend-Lease Act

Though Roosevelt had been cautiously providing material assistance to the Allies since the beginning of the war, the desperate situation in Europe in 1940 influenced the president to ask Congress for permission to provide all possible aid short of war to the Allies. In September, Roosevelt orchestrated the "destroyer for bases" deal with Great Britain, in which America lent Britain fifty desperately needed destroyers in exchange for leases on British possessions in the Western Hemisphere. In December 1940, following his successful campaign for an unprecedented third term (every president until Roosevelt kept with the tradition set by George Washington and did not seek more than two terms), during which he again pledged to the public that American troops would not be sent to Europe, President Roosevelt proposed a "Lend-Lease" program to provide supplies to Great Britain.

Opponents of the bill immediately charged that the Lend-Lease Act would lead the United States into active participation in the conflict. Senator Burton K. Wheeler of Montana charged that the Lend-Lease Act was nothing more than "a bill to enable the President to fight an undeclared war on Germany."[15] Wheeler and other opponents of the bill argued that in order for American supplies to reach Britain, American warships would have to be assigned convoy duty. That meant putting American ships and American lives in the line of fire and it increased the possibility of an armed exchange between German and U.S. naval forces. Despite vehement opposition, Congress passed the Lend-Lease Act in March 1941.

The use of American ships to convoy Lend-Lease supplies to Britain did indeed result in violent incidents between German and U.S. ships on a number of occasions. On September 4, 1941, the U.S. destroyer *Greer* exchanged fire with a German submarine. After the incident, Roosevelt ordered all American warships to shoot German warships on sight. On October 17, 1941, the USS *Kearny* was hit by German torpedoes near Greenland. Eleven American sailors were killed in the attack, and on October 31, 1941, a German submarine torpedoed the U.S. destroyer *Reuben James*. Roosevelt declared an unlimited national emergency and many felt that war with Germany was now inevitable. To everyone's shock, it was Japan, Germany's Axis ally in Asia, that provided the impetus for America's entry into the war and not Germany.

Pearl Harbor

Relations between the U.S. and Japan had been deteriorating since Japan's invasions of Manchuria in 1931 and China in 1937. With the fall of France and the Netherlands to Germany in 1940, Japan, desperately needing raw mate-

The Japanese attacked Pearl Harbor on December 7, 1941 in response to FDR's freezing of all Japanese assets and his insisting that Japan relinquish its claims in China and Southeast Asia.

rials to continue its campaign of conquest, began to covet French and Dutch colonial possessions in Asia. In response to Japanese aggression in the South Pacific and China, the U.S. government imposed an embargo of oil and scrap metal on Japan in July 1940. These sanctions were broadened in July 1941, when Roosevelt froze all Japanese assets in the United States. Negotiations between the two nations foundered when Roosevelt insisted that Japan relinquish all of its territorial claims in China and Southeast Asia. Feeling that they had been backed into a corner by American demands, the Japanese government chose to launch a preemptive attack upon the U.S. Pacific Fleet at Pearl Harbor, Hawaii. On December 8, 1941, one day after Japanese planes had nearly wiped out the entire U.S. Pacific Fleet, Congress passed a declaration of war against Japan. Three days later Germany declared war on the United States.

Criticism of Roosevelt's Policies

The Japanese attack and the German declaration of war ended the debate between Roosevelt and the isolationist segment of the public and Congress. The entire nation rallied behind the president once more and committed itself to total American victory at all costs. Roosevelt's actions leading up to the Japanese attack, however, still remain a source of debate.

Some observers contend that Roosevelt intended to take America into the war all along. Political commentator Patrick J. Buchanan argues that Roosevelt's policies of aiding Germany's enemies and forcing Japan to accept harsh American demands in Southeast Asia were devised with the intent of maneuvering Germany and its Axis allies into firing the first shot. Moreover, Buchanan argues, Germany did not represent a real threat to the United States after the Luftwaffe lost the Battle of Britain. According to Buchanan, if "the Luftwaffe could not achieve air superiority over the [English] Channel, how was it going to achieve it over the

Atlantic? If Hitler could not put a soldier into England in the fall of 1940, the notion that he could invade the Western Hemisphere . . . was preposterous."[16]

History professor William L. O'Neill, however, argues that Hitler and his Axis allies did indeed represent a potent threat to America and the rest of the world, and that President Roosevelt was justified in meeting that threat:

> All one can say in the end is that the war was, and remains, well worth the effort and the heartbreak. As evidence, one has only to imagine what kind of world we would live in today if America had remained neutral. Russia might have survived in a shrunken form, and Great Britain for a time also, but the rest of Eurasia would have been enslaved by the Axis powers. The Holocaust would have gone on to its bitter end, and we can be sure that a victorious Hitler, armed soon with atomic weapons and ballistic missiles, would have caused additional havoc—dwarfing that which was actually wreaked.[17]

Refugees and Evacuees

Roosevelt's handling of two groups of minorities during World War II—Jewish refugees from Hitler's Reich and Japanese Americans living on the West Coast of the United States—has also drawn criticism from historians. The Nazis had been openly persecuting Jews since Hitler came to power in 1933. On November 9, 1938, Nazi officials incited a nationwide night of anti-Jewish rioting in which synagogues and Jewish-owned property were destroyed. Countless Jews were killed and injured and tens of thousands were herded into concentration camps. The night became known as *Kristallnacht* (Night of the Broken Glass)— named for the shattered glass windows of Jewish-owned shops—and it provoked worldwide protest. The virulent anti-Semitism in Germany horrified President Roosevelt and in a November 15 press conference he condemned the

Although immigration quotas were in force after the Great Depression, FDR found ways of allowing many refugees from Nazi Germany into the United States.

Nazi regime, saying that he "could scarcely believe that such things could occur in a twentieth-century civilization."[18] Roosevelt was much more cautious in his approach to the Jewish refugees fleeing Nazi persecution, however.

As a result of the economic hard times brought on by the Great Depression, the United States had administered drastic immigration quotas. Most feared that immigrants would compete for scarce jobs and immigration restrictionists in Congress opposed raising the quota of foreigners allowed into the country for any reason. In 1938 150,000 people who sought to escape from Nazi Germany applied for visas, while the annual quota was just 27,370. Between July and December of 1940, when the demand for visas had reached its peak, the State Department issued only 22,508 visas.

Roosevelt never seriously challenged the immigration quotas. He did, however, work tirelessly to find safe havens for refugees fleeing from the Nazis, either in the United States or in other countries. Roosevelt also found some ways of getting around the quota system. Reasoning that it was now one country, the president combined the quotas from Germany and Austria when Germany annexed that country. Roosevelt also permitted refugees to land in the U.S. Virgin Islands as vacationers. Through a loophole in immigration law, the refugees could claim residence after a short stay and then proceed to the United States.

Though the United States accepted twice as many refugees as all other countries combined and Roosevelt applied constant pressure to the Allies to accept as many refugees as possible, some historians argue that Roosevelt's refugee policy was too cautious. While praising the president for his anti-fascist stance, Robert Edwin Herzstein nevertheless argues that "no excuse can be given for Roosevelt's calculated timidity"[19] involving Jewish refugees.

America's Concentration Camps

The destruction of the American Pacific Fleet by the Japanese left many citizens on the West Coast of the United States living in fear of a Japanese attack. So swift and decisive had the Japanese attack at Pearl Harbor been that many in the United States came to believe that the Japanese forces were aided by "fifth column" saboteurs of Japanese ancestry. Residents in California, Oregon, and Washington were overcome by a wave of anti-Japanese hysteria. Fear of fifth column activity on the West Coast was reinforced by respected journalist Walter Lippmann. In his nationally syndicated column, he charged that the Pacific Coast was in "imminent danger of a combined attack from within and from without."[20] Lippmann advocated the removal from the West Coast of the 110,000 people of Japanese descent—most of whom were American citizens by birth. Prominent California politicians such as Governor Culbert Olson, Attorney General Earl Warren (later to become Chief Justice of the United States), Los Angeles mayor Fletcher Bowron, and General John DeWitt, head of the army's Western Defense Command, agitated for the removal of Japanese Americans from the Pacific Coast. On February 19, 1942, despite evidence of their loyalty to the United States contained in a State Department investigation conducted by Curtis B. Munson, the president authorized the removal of all Japanese Americans from the West Coast when he signed Executive Order 9066. The evacuees were sent to relocation camps in the southwest where they remained until 1945.

A majority of observers maintain that the forced relocation of American citizens of Japanese descent is a black mark on the history of the United States and the record of Franklin D. Roosevelt. In 1980 Congress created the Commission on Wartime Relocation and Internment of Civilians to review the circumstances surrounding Executive Order 9066. The Commission's report, entitled *Personal Justice Denied* concluded that the actions taken against Japanese Americans by the military and President Roosevelt were not justified. Moreover, the report stated:

> The broad historical causes which shaped these decisions were race prejudice, war hysteria, and a failure of political leadership. . . . A grave injustice was done to American citizens and resident aliens of Japanese ancestry who, without individual review or any probative evidence against them, were excluded, removed and detained by the United States during World War II.[21]

Others, however, assert that a fair judgment cannot be assessed on Roosevelt's actions by those with the advantage of hindsight. The destruction of the Pacific Fleet left the West Coast of the United States virtually defenseless and vulnerable to attack. According to former evacuee Kiyoaki

Murata, "Given the military situation in 1942 it is understandable that the Army took every possible precaution to protect the West Coast. With the advantage of hindsight, it is easy now . . . to criticize the removal program."[22]

The President's Death

As the Allied armies closed in on victory in Europe and Southeast Asia, Franklin Roosevelt—despite rapidly failing health—defeated New York governor Thomas E. Dewey in the election of 1944 to win his fourth term as president. Roosevelt was the first and the last president to be elected to more than two terms. In 1951, the Twenty-Second Amendment, which prohibits a person from seeking more than two terms as president, was added to the Constitution. Roosevelt, however, did not live to finish his fourth term. On April 12, 1945, while taking a much-needed vacation at Warm Springs, President Roosevelt suffered a

FDR died of a massive cerebral hemorrhage on April 12, 1945, five months before the end of World War II, and before his fourth term of office could be completed.

massive cerebral hemorrhage and died. Funeral services were held in the White House and his body was carried by train to be buried in the Roosevelt family home in Hyde Park, New York.

The task of seeing the Allies through to victory fell to Vice President Harry S. Truman. Less than one month after Roosevelt's death, Adolf Hitler committed suicide in his Berlin bunker and Germany surrendered. Japan fought on until atomic bombs were dropped on Hiroshima and Nagasaki. On September 2, 1945, the Japanese signed the final surrender terms aboard the battleship *Missouri*.

Life in modern America is still very much a product of Franklin Roosevelt's twelve years in the White House. From America's leading role in the international order, to Social Security and the Securities and Exchange Commission, the revolutionary changes that Roosevelt effected in America's international and domestic affairs are still evident. Historians and political commentators continue to debate whether or not these changes were for the better. Some still argue that Roosevelt is guilty of creating the modern welfare state—an ungainly, inefficient, and expensive bureaucracy. Others counter that he not only saved democracy in America, he saved it in the rest of the world as well.

Notes

1. Quoted in Samuel I. Rosenman, ed., *The Public Papers and Addresses of Franklin D. Roosevelt*. New York: Random House, 1938, vol. 2, p. 11.

2. Nathan Miller, *F.D.R.: An Intimate History*. New York: Meridian, 1984, p. 15.

3. Quoted in Ted Morgan, *FDR: A Biography*. New York: Simon and Schuster, 1985, p. 23.

4. Quoted in Richard Thayer Goldberg, *The Making of Franklin D. Roosevelt: Triumph Over Disability*. Cambridge, MA: ABT Books, p. 9.

5. Quoted in Miller, *F.D.R.: An Intimate History*, p. 35.

6. Quoted in Morgan, *F.D.R.: A Biography*, pp. 155–56.

7. Quoted in Frank Freidel, *Franklin D. Roosevelt: A Rendezvous with Destiny.* Boston: Little, Brown, 1990, p. 26.

8. Quoted in Miller, *F.D.R.: An Intimate History,* p. 197.

9. Quoted in Morgan, *F.D.R.: A Biography,* p. 291.

10. Quoted in Morgan, *F.D.R.: A Biography,* p. 321.

11. John T. Flynn, *The Roosevelt Myth.* New York: Devin-Adair, 1956, p. 426.

12. Quoted in Don Nardo, ed., *Turning Points in World History: The Great Depression.* San Diego: Greenhaven Press, 2000, p. 107.

13. Harvard Sitkoff, *A New Deal for Blacks: The Emergence of Civil Rights as a National Issue: The Depression Decade.* New York: Oxford University Press, 1978, p. 44.

14. Kenneth S. Davis, *FDR: Into the Storm 1937–1940.* New York: Random House, 1993, p. 99.

15. Quoted in Flynn, *The Roosevelt Myth,* p. 295.

16. Patrick J. Buchanan, *A Republic, Not an Empire: Reclaiming America's Destiny.* Washington, DC: Regnery, 1999, p. 278.

17. Quoted in William Dudley, ed., *World War II: Opposing Viewpoints.* San Diego: Greenhaven Press, 1997, p. 247.

18. Quoted in Freidel, *Franklin D. Roosevelt: A Rendezvous with Destiny,* p. 314.

19. Robert Edwin Herzstein, *Roosevelt & Hitler: Prelude to War.* New York: Paragon, p. 237.

20. Walter Lippmann, "The Fifth Column on the Coast," *Los Angeles Times,* February 12, 1942.

21. Quoted in Roger Daniels, Sandra C. Taylor, and Harry H.L. Kitano, eds., *Japanese Americans: From Relocation to Redress.* Salt Lake City: University of Utah Press, 1986, p. 5.

22. Quoted in Lillian Baker, ed., *Dishonoring America: The Collective Guilt of American Japanese.* Lawndale, CA: Americans for Historical Accuracy, 1988, p. 23.

PRESIDENTS
and their
DECISIONS

THE NEW DEAL

THE THIRD AMERICAN REVOLUTION

CARL N. DEGLER

Since its declaration of independence from Britain, the United States has endured two cataclysmic events that reshaped the way Americans viewed their government. The first was the Civil War; the second was the Great Depression. According to Stanford University history professor Carl N. Degler, the New Deal—Franklin Roosevelt's collection of legislation designed to pull America from the depths of the depression—constituted a third American Revolution because it completely altered American thinking on the responsibilities of government. Until the depression, American government was dominated by the laissez-faire philosophy—a doctrine whose dominant themes were limited government power and involvement in the national economy and the welfare of its citizens. Degler writes that the miserable hardships endured during the Great Depression inspired the rejection of laissez-faire policies and convinced Americans of the necessity of federal involvement in the economy and the lives of the people.

———■———

Twice since the founding of the Republic, cataclysmic events have sliced through the fabric of American life, snapping many of the threads which ordinarily bind the past to the future. The War for the Union was one such event, the Great Depression of the 1930's the other. And, as the Civil War was precipitated from the political and moral

Excerpted from *Out of Our Past: The Forces That Shaped Modern America*, by Carl N. Degler. Copyright ©1959 by Carl N. Degler. Reprinted by permission of HarperCollins Publishers, Inc.

tensions of the preceding era, so the Great Depression was a culmination of the social and economic forces of industrialization and urbanization which had been transforming America since 1865. A depression of such pervasiveness as that of the thirties could happen only to a people already tightly interlaced by the multitudinous cords of a machine civilization and embedded in the matrix of an urban society.

In all our history no other economic collapse brought so many Americans to near starvation, endured so long, or came so close to overturning the basic institutions of American life. It is understandable, therefore, that from that experience should issue a new conception of the good society. . . .

The End of Laissez-Faire

Perhaps the most striking alteration in American thought which the depression fostered concerned the role of the government in the economy. Buffeted and bewildered by the economic debacle, the American people in the course of the 1930's abandoned, once and for all, the doctrine of laissez-faire. This beau ideal of the nineteenth-century economists had become, ever since the days of Jackson, an increasingly cherished shibboleth of Americans. But now it was almost casually discarded. It is true, of course, that the rejection of laissez-faire had a long history; certainly the Populists worked to undermine it. But with the depression the nation at large accepted the government as a permanent influence in the economy.

Almost every one of the best-known measures of the federal government during the depression era made inroads into the hitherto private preserves of business and the individual. Furthermore, most of these new measures survived the period, taking their places as fundamental elements in the structure of American life. For modern Americans living under a federal government of transcendent influence and control in the economy, this is the historic meaning of the Great Depression.

Much of what is taken for granted today as the legitimate function of government and the social responsibility of business began only with the legislation of these turbulent years. Out of the investigation of banking and bankers in 1933, for example, issued legislation which separated commercial banking from the stock and bond markets, and insured the bank deposits of ordinary citizens. The stock market, like the banks, was placed under new controls and a higher sense of responsibility to the public imposed upon it by the new Securities and Exchange Commission. The lesson of Black Tuesday in 1929 had not been forgotten; the classic free market itself—the Exchange—was hereafter to be under continuous governmental scrutiny.

The Government and Agriculture

The three Agricultural Adjustment Acts of 1933, 1936, and 1938, while somewhat diverse in detail, laid down the basic lines of what is still today the American approach to the agricultural problem. Ever since the collapse of the boom after the First World War, American agriculture had suffered from the low prices born of the tremendous surpluses. Unable to devise a method for expanding markets to absorb the excess, the government turned to restriction of output as the only feasible alternative. But because restriction of output meant curtailment of income for the farmer, it became necessary, if farm income was to be sustained, that farmers be compensated for their cut in production. Thus was inaugurated the singular phenomenon, which is still a part of the American answer to the agricultural surplus, of paying farmers for *not* growing crops. The other device introduced for raising farm prices, and still the mainstay of our farm policy, came with the 1938 act, which provided that the government would purchase and store excess farm goods, thus supporting the price level by withdrawing the surplus from the competitive market. Both methods constitute a subsidy for the farmer from society at large. . . .

Perhaps the most imaginative and fruitful innovation arising out of the depression was the Tennessee Valley Authority (TVA), which transformed the heart of the South. "It was and is literally a down to earth experiment," native Tennesseean Broadus Mitchell has written, "with all that we know from test tube and logarithm tables called on to help. It was a union of heart and mind to restore what had been wasted. It was a social resurrection." For the TVA was much more than flood and erosion control or even hydroelectric power—though its gleaming white dams are perhaps its most striking and best-known monuments. It was social planning of the most humane sort, where even the dead were carefully removed from cemeteries before the waters backed up behind the dams. It brought new ideas, new wealth, new skills, new hope into a wasted, tired, and discouraged region. . . .

Social Security

Undoubtedly Social Security deserves the appellation "revolutionary" quite as much as the TVA; it brought government into the lives of people as nothing had since the draft and the income tax. The original Social Security legislation actually comprised two systems: insurance against old age and insurance in the event of loss of work. The first system was completely organized and operated by the federal government; the second was shared with the states—but the national government set the standards; both were clear acknowledgment of the changes which had taken place in the family and in the business of making a living in America. No longer in urban America could the old folks, whose proportion in the society was steadily increasing, count on being taken in by their offspring as had been customary in a more agrarian world. Besides, such a makeshift arrangement was

Challenging the Policies of the Past

In the following excerpt, John Franklin Carter, an author who wrote under the pseudonym "Unofficial Observer," describes how Franklin Roosevelt successfully challenged the belief that government was powerless to alleviate the misery of the depression.

The country under Hoover was in utter despair, sunk in a moral apathy so profound that it was practically a coma. Unemployment was increasing, banks were failing, suffering and want were on every side and *nothing could be done about anything.* Crime, kidnapping, liquor lawlessness, moral disintegration coming on the heels of economic collapse, had made America a social shambles, in which the looter and the lawyer were kings. For nearly a generation the public had been taught that it was criminal folly to believe that political action offered any direct relief from economic distress. Our economists had taught that there was a tragic necessity for our economic breakdown and that it was impossible for

scarcely satisfying to the self-respect of the oldsters. With the transformation of the economy by industrialization, most Americans had become helpless before the vagaries of the business cycle. As a consequence of the social forces which were steadily augmenting social insecurity, only collective action by the government could arrest the drift.

To have the government concerned about the security of the individual was a new thing. Keenly aware of the novelty of this aim in individualistic America, Roosevelt was careful to deny any serious departure from traditional paths. "These three great objectives—the security of the home, the security of livelihood, and the security of social insurance," he said in 1934, constitute "a minimum of the human brains to invent a means to distribute the wealth which human bodies could produce....

When Roosevelt came in, it was as though a door had been opened, or rather, it was as though a door had been open all the time but we had not noticed it. He proved that it *was* possible to try to do something about conditions. That was enough. We proceeded—and he helped us—to lay disrespectful hands on every single one of the idols of the past: the gold standard, the open shop, free competition, private banking and private profits. To know that there was no human institution which could not be altered or outlawed by political action was to give us hope. In effect, it gave us life, a collective life which had been paralysed by the doctrines and policies of the past. By putting himself and his office at the service of the public will, Roosevelt entered the ranks of the political prophets.

John Franklin Carter, *The New Dealers*. New York: Simon and Schuster, 1934.

---

promise that we can offer to the American people." But this, he quickly added, "does not indicate a change in values."...

Unemployment

Apart from being a minimum protection for the individual and society against the dry rot of industrial idleness, unemployment insurance is now recognized as one of the major devices for warding off another depression. Never again will the unemployed be left without any source of spendable income, as they often were during the Great Depression.

For the average man, the scourge of unemployment was the essence of the depression. Widespread unemployment, permeating all ranks and stations in society, drove the American people and their government into some of their most determined and deliberate departures from the hallowed policy of "hands off." But despite the determination, as late as 1938 the workless still numbered almost ten million—two thirds as great as in 1932 under President Hoover. The governmental policies of the 1930's never appreciably diminished the horde of unemployed—only the war prosperity of 1940 and after did that—but the providing of jobs by the federal government was a reflection of the people's new conviction that the government had a responsibility to alleviate economic disaster. Such bold action on the part of government, after the ineffective, if earnest, approach of the Hoover administration, was a tonic for the dragging spirits of the people.

A whole range of agencies, from the Civil Works Administration (CWA) to the Works Progress Administration (WPA), were created to carry the attack against unemployment. It is true that the vast program of relief which was organized was not "permanent" in the sense that it is still in being, but for two reasons it deserves to be discussed here. First, since these agencies constituted America's principal weapon against unemployment, some form of them will surely be utilized if a depression should occur again. Second, the various relief agencies of the period afford the best examples of the new welfare outlook, which was then in the process of formation. . . .

Organized Labor

The Wagner Act broke new ground in labor law, going even beyond the epoch-making Norris–La Guardia Act of 1932. This latter act, passed after years of agitation and half a dozen tries on the part of labor and liberal congressmen and senators, severely restricted the use of antiunion injunctions issuing from federal courts in the course of labor disputes. So expertly was the act drawn that it overthrew in one stroke a mountain of legal obstacles to labor organization and activity which ingenious judges and lawyers had quarried out of the common law. In substance, though, the main achievement of the act could be summed up in the phrase "laissez-faire in labor relations." Labor would now be free to use its full economic power, without judicial hamstringing, just as employers had always been free to use theirs. In no way, it should be emphasized, did the Norris–La Guardia Act compel, or even advise, employers to accept unions or to bargain with them.

That innovation came only with the Wagner Act. As a federal court of appeals said in 1948, "prior to the National Labor Relations Act (NLRA) no federal law prevented *employers* from discharging employees for exercising their rights or from refusing to recognize or bargain with labor organizations. The NLRA created rights *against employ*ers which did not exist before then." In this lay the revolution in governmental attitudes toward organized labor. . . .

Was It a New or Old Deal?

One of the most enduring monuments to the Great Depression was that congeries of contradictions, naïveté, humanitarianism, realistic politics, and economic horse sense called the New Deal of Franklin D. Roosevelt. As the governmental agent which recast American thinking on the responsibilities of government, the New Deal was clearly the offspring of the depression. As we have seen, it was also more than that: it was a revitalization of the Democratic party; it was the political manifestation of that new spirit of reform which was stirring among the ranks of labor and black people. . . .

In the thirties, as now, the place of the New Deal in the broad stream of American development has been a matter of controversy. Historians and commentators on the American scene have not yet reached a firm agreement—if they ever will—as to whether the New Deal was conservative or radical in character. Certainly if one searches the writings and utterances of Franklin Roosevelt, his own consciousness of conservative aims is quickly apparent. "The New Deal is an old deal—as old as the earliest aspirations of humanity for liberty and justice and the good life," he declared in 1934. "It was this administration," he told a Chicago audience in 1936, "which saved the system of private profit and free enterprise after it had been dragged to the brink of ruin. . . ."

A Revolution of the Ballot Box

But those who are making a revolution among a profoundly conservative people do not advertise their activity, and above all, Franklin Roosevelt understood the temper of Americans. Only once during the 1932 campaign, Ernest K. Lindley has told us, did Roosevelt call for "a revolution"; and then he promptly qualified it to "the right kind, the only kind of revolution this nation can stand for—a revolution at the ballot box." Nor should such an interpretation be seen as an insinuation of high conspiracy— far from it. Roosevelt was a conservative at heart, as his lifelong interest in history, among other things, suggests. But he was without dogma in his conservatism, which was heavily interlaced with genuine concern for people. (When an economist suggested to F.D.R. that the depression be permitted to run its course and that then the economic system would soon right itself, the President's face took on a "gray look of horror" as he told the economist: "People aren't cattle, you know!") Roosevelt did not shy away from new means and new approaches to problems when circumstances demanded it. His willingness to experiment, to listen to his university-bred Brains Trust [a group of economic advisers], to accept a measure like the TVA, reveal the flexibility in his thought. Both his lack of theoretical presuppositions and his flexibility are to be seen in the way he came to support novel measures like Social Security and the Wagner Act. Response to popular demand was the

The depression-ridden American people saw Roosevelt, with his easygoing attitude and openness to new ideas, as a hopeful choice for the presidency in the election of 1932.

major reason. "The Congress can't stand the pressure of the Townsend Plan unless we have a real old-age insurance system," he complained to Frances Perkins, "nor can I face the country without having . . . a solid plan which will give some assurance to old people of systematic assistance upon retirement." In like manner, the revolutionary NLRA was adopted as a part of his otherwise sketchy and rule-of-thumb philosophy of society. Though ultimately Roosevelt championed the Wagner bill in the House, it was a belated conversion dictated by the foreshadowed success of the measure and the recent invalidation of the NRA. In his pragmatic and common-sense reactions to the exigencies of the depression, Roosevelt, the easy-going conservative, ironically enough became the embodiment of a new era and a new social philosophy for the American people.

"This election," Herbert Hoover presciently said in 1932, "is not a mere shift from the ins to the outs. It means deciding the direction our nation will take over a century to come." The election of Franklin Roosevelt, he predicted, would result in "a radical departure from the foundations of 150 years which have made this the greatest nation in the world." Though Hoover may be charged with nothing more than campaign flourishing, it is nevertheless a fact that his speech was made just after Roosevelt's revealing Commonwealth Club address of September. Only in this single utterance, it should be remembered, did Roosevelt disclose in clear outline the philosophy and program which was later to be the New Deal. "Every man has a right to life," he had said, "and this means that he has also a right to make a comfortable living. . . . Our government, formal and informal, political and economic," he went on, "owes to everyone an avenue to possess himself of a portion of that plenty [from our industrial society] sufficient for his needs, through his own work." Here were the intimations of those new goals which the New Deal set for America. . . .

Few areas of American life were beyond the touch of the experimenting fingers of the New Deal; even the once sacrosanct domain of prices and the valuation of money felt the tinkering. The devaluation of the dollar, the gold-purchase program, the departure from the gold standard—in short, the whole monetary policy undertaken by F.D.R. as a means to stimulate recovery through a price rise—constituted an unprecedented repudiation of orthodox public finance. To achieve that minimum standard of well-being which the depression had taught the American people to expect of their government, nothing was out of bounds.

But it is not the variety of change which stamps the New Deal as the creator of a new America; its significance lies in the expansion and permanence of its programs. In many ways, the Great Society of Lyndon Johnson was but the fulfilling of the implicit promises of the New Deal. Johnson himself began his spectacular career, appropriately enough, as a New Deal bureaucrat in the Texas office of the National Youth Administration; by 1937 he was a freshman Congressman from Texas fervently supporting F.D.R. As President himself in an age of prosperity, Johnson never let the nation forget his aim of carrying on in the tradition of Franklin Roosevelt and his New Deal. Johnson's own Great Society programs in behalf of education, urban renewal, medical care, housing, and other welfare programs may have gone beyond the New Deal in degree, but not in kind. In an age of affluence, the Great Society could assume costs that the depression-ridden New Deal could not, but the programs advanced by the Great Society were within the humanitarian guidelines laid down by the New Deal. The Great Society, in short, was the Guarantor State realized. Even Johnson's remarkable support of civil rights and the black revolution of the 1960's, for which there was, admittedly, no comparable plank in the New Deal's platform, can be viewed as a forthright extension of what, as we have seen, the New Deal had done in behalf of Negroes only indirectly. It is not accidental that to this day, almost half a century after the New Deal revolutionized the political allegiances of blacks, the Democratic party of Franklin Roosevelt, Lyndon Johnson, and Jimmy Carter continues to enjoy the support of the great preponderance of black voters.

There is another measure of the New Deal's significance in American social and political history. No Republican administration since then has repudiated the New Deal's essentials, not Eisenhower's, nor Nixon's, nor Ford's, nor Ronald Reagan's. Reagan, it is true, has lashed out against the growth in the power and size of the federal establishment, something for which the New Deal may be fairly held responsible for initiating. In his first State of the Union Address in January, 1982, Reagan made clear that it was indeed the New Deal that he held responsible. Proudly he told the country that "after fifty years of taking power away from the hands of the people in their states and local communities we have started returning power and resources to them." Yet even he was not prepared to tamper with Social Security, the National Labor Relations Act or even the limited socialism of the TVA. And ten years before Ronald Reagan entered the White House, Richard Nixon admitted that he had finally accepted the new Keynesian economics of deficit spending as part of the federal government's responsibility in regulating the economy and avoiding another depression. Nor has the Republican party in any of its national conventions since 1945 dared to advocate the repeal or even the emasculation of the vitals of the New Deal: TVA, SEC, AAA, Social Security, the Wagner Act, and the hours and wages laws. The New Deal Revolution has become so much a part of the American Way that no political party that aspires to office even dreams of repudiating it.

The conclusion seems inescapable that, traditional as the words may have been in which the New Deal expressed itself, in actuality it was truly a revolution in ideas, institutions and practices, when one compares it with the political and social world that preceded it. In its long history, America has passed through two revolutions since the first one in 1776, but only the last two, the Civil War and the depression, were of such force as to change the direction of the relatively smooth flow of its progress. The Civil War rendered a final and irrevocable decision in the long debate over the nature of the Union and the position of the Negro in American society. From that revolutionary experience, America emerged a strong national state and dedicated by the words of its most hallowed document to the inclusion of black people in a democratic culture. The searing ordeal of the Great Depression purged the American people of their belief in the limited powers of the federal government and convinced them of the necessity of the guarantor state. And as the Civil War constituted a watershed in American thought, so the depression and its New Deal marked the crossing of a divide from which, it would seem, there could be no turning back.

THE NEW DEAL MARKED THE BEGINNING OF THE WELFARE STATE

PAUL K. CONKIN

According to University of Wisconsin scholar Paul K. Conkin, the largest welfare program in American history began with the implementation of Franklin Roosevelt's New Deal. In his attempt to relieve the suffering of the needy and guard against future depressions by pouring massive amounts of government money into the economy—welfare for business—Franklin Roosevelt launched the modern welfare state. Though Roosevelt's welfare efforts provided some relief for the poor and provided some insurance for business, they did not eliminate poverty and they ultimately failed to fully revive America's ailing economy. Moreover, Roosevelt's relief efforts resulted in the largest accretion to the national debt at that time—almost five billion dollars—and fueled the growth of government bureaucracy.

T HE MISERY OF DEPRESSION MULTIPLIED THE NEED FOR PUB- lic welfare. The Democratic sweep in the election of 1934 created a favorable political climate for new federal action. Several New Deal agency heads had already worked out ambitious programs and waited hopefully for funds. Mounting public pressure, often fanned by nostrum-peddling demagogues, helped mute established inhibitions. The [Supreme] Court deathblow to the National Recovery Administration (N.R.A.) in 1935, plus congressional pres-

Excerpts (edited) reprinted, with permission, from *The New Deal*, 3rd ed., by Paul K. Conkin, pp. 54–56, 58–60, 66, 69, 71, 75–76, 80–82. Copyright ©1992 by Harlan Davidson, Inc.

sures, forced Roosevelt to seek a new labor policy, while bitter attacks from a majority of businessmen so angered him that he gladly turned to the working classes for political support. Finally, a growing number of his advisers accepted a monetary, budgetary approach to a still elusive recovery and thus welcomed the deficits involved in large relief programs. These pressures all converged on Congress in 1935, producing a new body of legislation that, with almost unbelievable speed, launched the American welfare state, a brand new, large, ungainly infant, destined to survive all the hazards of childhood and a maladjusted adolescence, eventually to mature in the Great Society, still ugly but increasingly popular.

Welfare Capitalism

The term "welfare state" has many connotations, accompanied by degrees of emotional approval or distaste. To a few Americans it is an antonym of freedom, a synonym of socialism, a repudiation of responsibility, a catalyst of character decline and civilization's rot. To others it connotes halfway, palliative measures, mere sops to the exploited in behalf of preserving privilege and unfair advantage. Rooted in the conservatism of a Bismarck, it is the complete antithesis of socialism. To a much larger group, it is an imperfect but necessary compromise between various contending forces and is thus the middle way, the moderate answer. Despite all the bitterness of the thirties, or even of the sixties, a type of welfare capitalism has become the established system in America, approved by a substantial majority of the voters. It is now conventional and orthodox, however much bolstered by an effective political appeal that still makes it sound progressive and daring, which it really never was.

In a loose way, everyone favors enhancing the general welfare. The problem is one of means. In the American past the key term was always opportunity, with a type of disciplined freedom closely connected. Governments had a crucial role—protecting and extending opportunity. In this sense, every good state was a welfare state. In a free society, with beckoning opportunities, with no special privileges, each individual or cooperative effort to take advantage of existing opportunities was conceived as a lesson in responsibility, as an inducement to good character, and as a fulfilling experience. Such a simple but profound faith lay at the moralistic heart of American politics. Private property, meaning the actual means of production, and free enterprise, meaning the private right to manage these means, were indispensable elements in this faith. In fact, they were at the heart of a moral society. Everyone should have an opportunity to own and manage, or at least to share in the owning and management, of productive property. But, to repeat a truism, the faith survived but not the sustaining environment. There was never as much opportunity as the faith presumed. By 1930 only a few people could own and manage property. In this sense opportunity disappeared. But an ersatz type of opportunity—to work for other men, to sell one's labor to those who did own and manage property—replaced an earlier dream of farm or shop, along with an ersatz type of property—common stock, or claims on profits but no real role in management. In the depression even these poor substitutes paled. Up to fifteen million family heads could find no market for their labor and had to turn either to private or public charity. . . .

Emergency Relief Appropriation

The largest welfare program of the New Deal, and of American history, began in 1935. A newly elected, exceedingly generous Congress approved a $4,880,000,000 Emergency Relief Appropriation, to be spent as Roosevelt saw fit. This was, up until this time, the largest appropriation in American history and the largest accretion to the national debt. It was used to consolidate and expand numerous early, temporary relief programs, which had served up to thirty million people. About $1,500,000,000, the largest single block, went to Harry Hopkins and to a new relief organization created by executive order, the huge Works Progress Administration (W.P.A.). In turn, the W.P.A. used most of its share, plus endless new appropriations, for work programs for the unemployed. At times its projects resembled those of the more reputable Public Works Administration (P.W.A.), even as a favored Hopkins cut into what [Secretary of the Interior and P.W.A. Administrator Harold] Ickes believed should have been his share of the appropriation. Against the wishes of congressional liberals, W.P.A. wages were generally scaled below those of private industry, and anyone offered private employment became ineligible for W.P.A. work. Burdened by a lack of developed plans for massive public works, by an oversupply of unskilled laborers, and by rigid rules, the W.P.A. was inefficient by any private standard. Nonetheless, the completed projects in part compensated for the money spent and represented a great gain over direct doles. Despite vigorous efforts to maintain high morale, and despite the sincere appreciation of most workers, the W.P.A. could not escape some of the stigma of relief. In fact, derisive opponents would not let it. Also, the W.P.A. could only employ about a third of those who needed work, leaving millions to the care or neglect of states. Many had to remain on a dole, often supplemented by free food distributed by a Federal Surplus Commodities Corporation. . . .

Social Security

The Social Security Act of 1935 became the supreme symbol of a welfare state. As enacted, it hardly deserved the honor or opprobrium. At most, it set some enduring precedents and established a new area of federal responsibility. As shown by Edwin E. Witte [*Development of the Social Security Act* (Madison, 1962)], the bill was tremendously complex, compromising many divergent plans and establishing an array of welfare programs. . . .

The Social Security Act set up the present compulsory tax for retirement benefits, a tax assessed in equal parts on employer and employee. About half of the people were excluded by the original act, including farmers, domestics, and the elderly. The employee tax represented a significant drain from already low payrolls and thus a further obstacle to recovery. The original act did not protect against accidents and illness before retirement, provided no medical insurance, and paid benefits on the basis of past earning instead of present needs. Thus, it was close to a compulsory insurance system, paid for largely by those who benefited. The unemployment insurance provision delegated most responsibility to the states and invited chaotic variations in always inadequate payments. Since the retirement coverage was so limited, the act provided matching federal funds for traditional state pensions for the aged and funds for dependent mothers, children, and the crippled and blind. The present public welfare system, although administered locally and almost always inadequate, is closely tied to this federal assistance. . . .

The welfare legislation, large in hopes generated, often pitifully small in actual benefits, hardly represented a social revolution. Except for relief, only a small burden had been added to the national budget, and none of the welfare programs significantly redistributed the wealth of the country. Not only [radical Louisiana Senator] Huey Long, but politicians of varied persuasions wanted to lessen disparities of income and accumulated wealth. Some Progressives, led by [Supreme Court Justice Louis D.] Brandeis and like foes of centralized power, also wanted to help restore competition by placing a tax burden on bigness. Roosevelt, enraged by hostile newspapers and by business criticism, increasingly advised by [future Supreme Court Justice] Felix Frankfurter (then at the Harvard Law School and a Brandeis disciple), and always thirsting for a good fight, presented Congress with a new and biting tax proposal in the spring of 1935. It had two purposes: a fairer sharing of the tax burden and penalties on large enterprise. The bill, soon labeled a "soak-the-rich" measure, provoked an embittered controversy. It marked the most decisive turn by Roosevelt from consensus politics to a clear appeal to the disinherited. The tax message rested on the depressing fact that, so far, New Deal policies had created a more regressive tax system, with greater burdens on consumption and low incomes than on large incomes. Large corporations had used the depression to reduce debts and to increase their liquid capital, even while suffering operating losses, suspending dividends, and thus avoiding taxes. Also, then as now, large incomes escaped existing tax schedules by loopholes and avoidance. . . .

The welfare measures and the battle against bigness were also related to the old problem of recovery. Since the largest welfare expenditures came from the borrowed appropriation of 1935, they provided a direct stimulus to increased consumption. But this stimulus was at least in part balanced by the insecurity of businessmen, who saw terrible apostasy in most relief measures and apocalyptic doom in the holding company and tax proposals. Roosevelt still yearned for a balanced budget but justified deficits on humane grounds. Several new advisers, such as Thomas Corcoran, a boyish but intellectually quick protégé of Frankfurter, seemed more concerned with penalizing big business than in achieving recovery. But one New Deal official, Marriner Eccles, a competent Utah economist and banker, viewed the depression very much as [British economist John Maynard] Keynes and worked assiduously for banking and spending policies conducive to recovery (which necessitated, among other things, an increase in business activity). More than anyone except [Rexford G.] Tugwell (who left the New Deal at the end of 1936), Eccles offered economic advice that, though much more pro-business, was logical and coherent. . . .

Beginning in 1935 there was a steady upturn in almost all economic indexes. The valley of depression began to rise slowly toward the foothills of recovery, a recovery which was too often conceived in the terms of 1929, as if continued growth was unthinkable. The weaknesses were obvious. Unemployment, after declining from the peak of 1933 (twelve to fifteen million), sunk to approximately eight million and stuck there. Consumer buying remained well below 1929. The construction industries were pitifully depressed at only one-fourth the high level of 1929. The economy had achieved an equilibrium of slow growth, sustained largely by relief expenditures. Yet the old idea of a mature economy persisted. Many New Dealers, including Roosevelt, were happy with the rising charts. In the campaign of 1936 he promised to battle against the remaining ills of the economy and against the selfish men who prevented full victory, and proudly took credit for having lifted America from depression. . . .

Since the New Deal failed to fulfill even the minimal dream of most reformers, why did all the evil men of power, plus millions of Republican dupes, oppose it? To Roosevelt, the answer was simple: they were evil. Economic royalists, with a monopoly of power, they were not content with a repaired and honest capitalism. Instead, they wanted to drive on with their plutocracy and bring down upon the heads of the good men of power the inevitable revolution. Then good bankers would suffer and good businessmen might lose the management of their corporations. But this answer, although in part true, was too simple. The opponents of Roosevelt misconstrued the direction of the New Deal. Many believed Roosevelt's class rhetoric. They really thought America was losing its "free" capitalist soul to some type of socialism. In their praise of freedom lurked some valuable criticism of the New Deal.

Also, many Americans, perhaps particularly the monied classes, never trusted Roosevelt, much less some of his advisers. The New Deal was indeed a mixed company, a type of political bohemia, frequented by many of the better sort, but still dangerous. Roosevelt was a puzzling creature. Even when he served conservative causes, he preached an alien gospel. Let us have anything but a righteous gentleman in Washington. Even a Marxist would have made more sense to them. Finally, almost no one thought in terms of vast economic expansion, and thus no one could see welfare as other than a permanent liability, somehow drawn from the ledger of profits or high incomes, either directly by taxes or indirectly by government deficits and inflation. The threat to earnings, the inhibition to investment, seemed the central issue, more important than declining fears of revolution, humane concern, or an occasional recognition of the importance of purchasing power.

But the supreme irony is here. The enemies of the New Deal were wrong. They should have been friends. Security was a prime concern of the insecure thirties. It cut across all classes. Businessmen, by their policies, desperately sought it in lowered corporate debts and tried to get the government to practice the same austerity. Even when ragged and ill-housed, workers opened savings accounts. The New Deal, by its policies, underwrote a vast apparatus of security. But the meager benefits of Social Security were insignificant in comparison to the building system of security for large, established businesses. But like stingy laborers, the frightened businessmen did not use and enjoy this security and thus increase it. The New Deal tried to frame institutions to protect capitalism from major business cycles and began in an unclear sort of way to underwrite continuous economic growth and sustained profits. Although some tax bills were aimed at high profits, there was no attack on fair profits or even on large profits. During the thirties, as all the way up to the sixties, there was no significant leveling by taxes. The proportionate distribution of wealth remained. Because of tax policies, even relief expenditures were disguised subsidies to corporations, since they were in large part paid by future taxes on individual salaries or on consumer goods. Thus, instead of higher wages creating a market, at the short-term expense of profits, the government subsidized the businessman, without taking the cost out of his hide as he expected and feared. . . .

The shift to welfare policies and then to Keynesian recovery policies took away most of the threat and left private interests shaken but more secure than ever. Nationalization and economic planning became dead issues. Through banking and budgetary policies the government's resources were to be used to protect, support, and occasionally discipline private producers. This meant a helping hand for private industry, but with too many obligations, too many secure guarantees, and too many restrictions for many old-fashioned industrialists. Security does reduce freedom.

But the government had, more clearly than ever in the past, committed itself to national economic goals. This was one of the enduring achievements of the New Deal. Since it rejected planning (except to a degree in agriculture) and refused to do its own producing, it had no alternative but to rely on the major corporations and to subsidize them if necessary to insure its goals of rapid growth, high levels of employment, and low welfare needs. Even a slight increase in private economic activity can do more to benefit the country than vast welfare programs. Precluded from direct economic action, the government had to use indirect controls and incentives, plus persuasion, bribes, or, if politically possible, threats and punitive measures. In this situation, high profits rightfully became desirable public policy, since they increased the total economic activity and the level of national prosperity. In spite of all the ridicule, nothing was now truer than the quip: "What is good for General Motors is good for the country." Under the emerging system, the welfare of both were inseparable.

The dependence was mutual. The large corporations, protected by a generous government against the insecurity of the past (when politicians could safely allow depressions) and also against their own worst mistakes and abuses, were tied to government policies. The national budget was almost as important as their corporate budgets. The action of the Federal Reserve Board, or even random pronouncements by government officials, could wreck their best-laid plans. Welfare spending became a small but marginally vital part of the total market for goods, forcing some business acquiescence even here. In a few areas, such as low-rent housing, welfare programs became the major support for very profitable businesses. Later, defense spending would completely support large companies and provide the margin of profit for hundreds. Increasingly, business and government were linked in more subtle ways, particularly by a common economic orthodoxy and a common need for certain skills. Bureaucrats moved from Ivy League campuses to corporations and on to Washington. The situation invited, in fact necessitated, co-operation, or a truly joint enterprise. Roosevelt cleared the way for such co-operation, but he never desired it or achieved it and probably never perceived its inescapable logic. Unlike most politicians, he was never a good businessman, nor could he share power easily.

The old, individualistic capitalist did not fit the new picture. Mavericks were taboo. But neither did reformers fit. The new partnership, with greater government participation and greater benefits (the welfare state for business), left room for tension, even bitter conflict, as between mutually dependent husband and wife. Always, one or the other partner could try to gain too much power and upset the partnership. There was an overlapping but never identical constituency. Generally, with time and enough advice from Keynesian counselors, the two settled into almost blissful matrimony. Lyndon Johnson finally illustrated what a beautiful and happy home is possible when both sides can sit down and reason together. What about the constituency? For business, the shareholders have profited. Dividends have been large and capital accumulation even larger. For government, the larger constituency presents a much more variegated pattern. But most able and fortunate people, if they have been loyal, have received well in material returns and have profited from the general benevolence and good will of both the private and government bureaucrats who look out for them.

But the economic magic of sustained growth and the political magic of welfare can be irrelevant to moral and religious vision, which may also demand a just community. For the more sensitive New Dealers, or outside critics, Keynes provided a technique for priming the economic pump but no means of purifying the water. They thirsted after the pure product. Growth could simply intoxicate the affluent minority (or majority), blunt their sensitivity, and leave them in satiated lethargy, full but unfulfilled. Welfare could do the same for the poor. Growth could lead to vast production, to an enormous gross national product, but also to ugliness and spiritual poverty everywhere. It might even lead to full employment and undreamed-of security (goals not attained because of too small a government investment), yet to a society bereft of meaningful work, of personal involvement, even of democratic participation. It might suggest the blessing of leisure but bring only the curse of idleness. Finally, it would surely conceal injustice and leave the exploited to the tender and prejudiced mercy of local conscience. During the war the disturbing reformers dropped from view and did not emerge again until the sixties. Then, to the profound surprise of all good men of power, the one-third ill-fed and ill-housed, and the two-thirds alienated and desperate, still existed. In spite of the New Deal and in spite of all that welfare!

THE NEW DEAL ROOSEVELT PROMISED VS. THE ONE HE DELIVERED

JOHN T. FLYNN

When Franklin Roosevelt was campaigning for the presidency in 1932 he described to the voters a program that would alleviate the debilitating effects of the depression without providing direct handouts to the needy, creating a budget deficit, or increasing government expenditures. The New Deal that Roosevelt preached was a sound economic policy that fit within the traditional framework of American government, with an emphasis on states' rights, opposition to an overly powerful central government, and opposition to deficit spending. In the following essay, John T. Flynn, a journalist during Roosevelt's terms in office, describes how Roosevelt implemented a very different New Deal after he assumed the presidency. With this "second" New Deal Roosevelt repudiated the principles he preached during the campaign and created a government that dwarfed all previous administrations in size and expenditure.

I N THE BEGINNING, OF COURSE, WAS ROOSEVELT. AND THEN came the Brain Trust [Roosevelt's economic advisers]. After that we had the Great Man and the Brain Trust. The casual reader may suppose this is just a catchy collection of syllables. But it is impossible to estimate the power these few words exercised upon the minds of the American people. After all, a crowd of big business boobies, a lot of butter-fingered politicians, two big halls full of shallow and stupid congressmen and senators had made a mess of America. That was the bill of goods sold to the American people. Now amidst the ruins appeared not a mere politician, not a crowd of tradesmen and bankers and congressmen, but a Great Man attended by a Brain Trust to bring understanding first and then order out of chaos. . . .

New Deal Promises

To meet the country's ills, the New Deal made certain pledges, which described how Roosevelt would save the country.

It would relieve the needy—but no doles. The government would prepare a program of useful public works, such as flood control, soil and forest protection and necessary public buildings. But it would immediately put a million men to work in the forests. This alone would provide the necessary employment. Where public works were self-liquidating—that is where they would pay for themselves—they could be financed by bond issues. But where they were not they must be paid for by taxes. Beyond that, the New Deal would seek to shorten the work week and reduce hours of labor to spread employment.

For the farmer the New Deal would encourage cooperatives and enlarge government lending agencies. But the greatest enemy of the farmer was his habit of producing too much. His surplus ruined his prices. The New Deal would contrive means of controlling the surplus and ensuring a profitable price. But it denounced any proposals to have the federal government go into the market to purchase and speculate in farm products in a futile attempt to increase prices or reduce farm surpluses.

As for business the New Deal proposed strict enforcement of the anti-trust laws, full publicity about security offerings, regulation of holding companies which sell securities in interstate commerce, regulation of rates of utility companies operating across state lines and the regulation of the stock and commodity exchanges.

But greatest of all—the New Deal promised economy. The extravagance of the Hoover administration, its yearly deficits—these were at the bottom of all our ills. The New Deal would abolish useless bureaus, reduce salaries, cut federal expenditures 25 per cent. The New Deal would put an end to government borrowing—it would end the deficits. The New Deal would assure a sound currency at all hazards and finally a competitive tariff with a tariff commission free from presidential interference.

A Standard Democratic Platform

There was nothing revolutionary in all this. It was a platform that Woodrow Wilson might have endorsed. It was actually an old-time Democratic platform based upon fairly well-accepted principles of the traditional Democratic party. That party had always denounced the tendency to strong central government, the creation of new bureaus. It had always denounced deficit financing. Its central principle of action was a minimum of government in business. The government might intervene, as in the anti-trust laws, not to manage business or tell business what it should do, but to prevent business from engaging in practices which interfered with the free action of others. It made war upon those who attempted to impose restraints upon commerce. It was always for a competitive tariff, save for the products of the Southern states which needed protection. And it always proclaimed loudly its solicitude for labor and for the "common man." It always attacked Wall Street, the Stock Exchange, the big bankers.

Mr. Roosevelt in his pre-election speeches had stressed all these points—observing the rights of the states so far as to urge that relief, old-age pensions and unemployment insurance should be administered by them, that the federal government would merely aid the states with relief

Many of Roosevelt's speeches to the American people contained the same basic themes. He often talked of less government spending and no deficits.

funds and serve as collection agent for social insurance. And above all he rang the changes upon the shocking spendings of the Republicans and the mounting public debt. He called Herbert Hoover "the greatest spender in history." He cried out against the Republican party: "It has piled bureau on bureau, commission on commission . . . at the expense of the taxpayer." He told the people: "For three long years I have been going up and down this country preaching that government—federal, state and local—costs too much. I shall not stop that preaching." The statement is a curious one, since I can find among his published addresses while he was governor up until the time of his nomination, not one reference to government deficits. And for a good reason, of course, since as governor he took New York State from the hands of Al Smith with a surplus of $15,000,000 and left it with a deficit of $90,000,000. He was against Big Government. "We must eliminate the functions of government . . . we must merge, we must consolidate subdivisions of government and, like private citizens, give up luxuries which we can no longer afford."

"Stop the Deficits!"

He repeated this over and over: "I propose to you that government, big and little, be made solvent and that the example be set by the President of the United States and his cabinet." Toward the end of the campaign he cried: "Stop the deficits! Stop the deficits!" Then to impress his listeners with his inflexible purpose to deal with this prodigal monster, he said: "Before any man enters my cabinet he must give me a twofold pledge: Absolute loyalty to the Democratic platform and especially to its economy plank. And complete cooperation with me in looking to economy and reorganization in his department."

This was the New Deal as it was described to the people in the fall of 1932. Practically any Democrat could subscribe to it. The only slightly radical feature was his declaration about government development of water power. But he was merely following the lead of Al Smith and he assured the people that he believed in private ownership and development of water power with the exception of Muscle Shoals [Alabama] and perhaps three others merely to be yardsticks as a means of checking the rates of private companies.

This New Deal was a program for action strictly within the framework of the traditional American system of government, with emphasis on states' rights, opposition to too powerful central government, opposition to BIG government which should be cut down to its proper size, opposition to high taxes, unbalanced budgets, government debts. Where the name New Deal came from I do not know. Stuart Chase had written a book called *A New Deal* some time before in which he outlined a completely different program. Perhaps the name was swiped from this book. But in any case the Roosevelt New Deal was as I have described it. This was what the people voted for in 1932. Now Mr. Roosevelt, in March, 1933, was in the White House. And there he proceeded to set up what he continued to call the New Deal. How much did it resemble the one voted on in November, 1932?

A New New Deal

In the first hundred days of his administration, Mr. Roosevelt put into effect a program of very large dimensions. But it was a program built on a wholly different principle from that which was described as the New Deal.

First of all, his central principle—his party's traditional principle of war upon BIG government—was reversed. And he set out to build a government that in size dwarfed the government of Hoover which he denounced.

The idea of a government that was geared to assist the economic system to function freely by policing and preventive interference in its freedom was abandoned for a government which upon an amazing scale undertook to organize every profession, every trade, every craft under its supervision and to deal directly with such details as the volume of production, the prices, the means and methods of distribution of every conceivable product. This was the National Recovery Administration (NRA). It may be that this was a wise experiment but it was certainly the very reverse of the kind of government which Mr. Roosevelt proposed in his New Deal.

Enforcement of the anti-trust act was a long-time pet of his party and it was considered as an essential instrument to prevent cartels and trusts and combinations in restraint of trade which were supposed to be deadly to the system of free enterprise. The New Deal had called

Roosevelt Tries to
Explain an Inconsistency

Fireside chats were frequent addresses that Roosevelt delivered over the radio during his presidency. The following excerpt is taken from Roosevelt's fireside chat of July 24, 1933, in which the president attempts to explain how he will cut government expenditures while spending unprecedented billions for emergency relief measures.

Long before Inauguration Day I became convinced that individual effort and local effort and even disjointed Federal effort had failed and of necessity would fail and, therefore, that a rounded leadership by the Federal Government had become a necessity both of theory and of fact. Such leadership, however, had its beginning in preserving and strengthening the credit of the United States Government, because without that no leadership was a possibility. For years the Government had not lived within its income. The immediate task was to bring our regular expenses within our revenues. That has been done. It may seem inconsistent for a government to cut down its regular expenses and at the same time to borrow and to spend billions for an emergency. But it is not inconsistent because a large portion of the emergency money has been paid out in the form of sound loans which will be repaid to the Treasury over a period of years; and to cover the rest of the emergency money we have imposed taxes to pay the interest and the installments on that part of the debt.

So you will see that we have kept our credit good. We have built a granite foundation in a period of confusion. That foundation of the Federal credit stands there broad and sure. It is the base of the whole recovery plan.

Franklin D. Roosevelt, Fireside Chat, Monday, July 24, 1933, 9:30 P.M.

loudly for its strict enforcement. Yet almost at once it was suspended—actually put aside during the experiment—in order to cartelize every industry in America on the Italian corporative model.

The Deficit

That deadly thing, the deficit, which, as he had said was at the bottom of all our woes and which stemmed from big government and extravagant government, was not slain as Roosevelt had proposed. Instead it was adopted and fed and fattened until it grew to such proportions that Hoover began to look like a niggard. The theory that relief should be carried on by the states was abandoned. The idea of self-liquidating public works was abandoned and all forms of relief were carried on by public loans, adding to the national debt. The idea of useful public works was abandoned in favor of hurriedly devised "make-work" which was nothing more than a disguised dole.

The "spendthrift" Hoover had increased his expenditures by 50 per cent in four years over the 1927 level. In four years Mr. Roosevelt increased his 300 per cent over the 1927 level and to 100 per cent over Hoover's. Stop the deficits! Stop the deficits! he had cried. Instead of stopping them he ended his first term with a deficit of 15 billion dollars.

I am not here criticizing what Mr. Roosevelt did. I merely want to fix clearly the fact that what he did was the reverse of what he had described as a New Deal.

When the President had declared for a "sound currency at all hazards" he was using a phrase well-known to describe a currency based on gold. Yet one of his earliest acts was to go off the gold standard and to declare later for a managed currency based on the commodity dollar.

Had a candidate opposing Mr. Roosevelt in the campaign declared that he favored that series of policies and projects which Roosevelt launched when he came to power, there is not the slightest doubt that Roosevelt would have covered him with damnation and ridicule. Actually he did denounce Mr. Hoover who, Roosevelt charged, had asked the farmers to plow under every third row of wheat, cotton and corn and he did denounce and ridicule what he described as attempts by the government to go into the market and speculate in commodities in order to raise prices. Yet he not only asked farmers to plow under the crops but he paid them to do so and ended by compelling them to do so in effect, and his agents were in every market place to purchase crops in order to fix prices—not merely in the grain exchanges and cotton exchanges, but in every kind of exchange and market covering every conceivable crop from eggs and poultry to sweet potatoes, peanuts, apples and applesauce.

Why?

Why did the President completely reverse his policy after his inauguration? It must be because he felt the things he was urging before election were not adapted to the realities of the case when he came to power. When he was outlining his policies before election he was completely cocksure of his rectitude and wisdom. Yet all those policies and techniques of which he was so absolutely certain he brushed aside as unusable. What became of his announced intention to demand from every cabinet member two pledges: (1) to abide absolutely by the Democratic platform and (2) to cooperate with him in cutting down the expenses of the departments? He began by cutting expenses 25 per cent. But before the ink was dry on that act he had thrown it into the ashcan with a $3,300,000,000 deficit in the NRA act. And no cabinet member expanded the costs of his department more than the President himself expanded the costs of the Presidential budget.

When was Mr. Roosevelt right? When he was making speeches before the election or when he was acting after the election? We need not accuse him of dishonesty either time. We may say in tolerance that he laid down in perfect honesty a policy when he was a candidate and that when he found himself in Hoover's place he found his first New Deal unsuited to the needs of the time. But we cannot say that the thing called the New Deal in 1932 was the same as the thing which he called the New Deal from 1933 to 1936. He pronounced a definite judgment upon the New Deal he presented so gaudily before the election by completely repudiating it when he became President. It was one thing to challenge Hoover and to abuse him. Faced with the demands of power, he had to confess by his course that the policy he had outlined before the election was a mistake. I do not say it was a mistake. Which policy was nearest right is a question yet to be answered.

At the end of the One Hundred Days Mr. Roosevelt was embarked upon a new New Deal. There were happy young men in Washington bureaus who were calling it the Roosevelt Revolution, and soon we would hear that term in wide use. Others began to call it the Second New Deal. And that is precisely what it was—essentially and in detail, save for a few minor matters, a wholly different thing.

CRITICISM OF THE NEW DEAL IS NOT JUSTIFIED

GEORGE WOLFSKILL AND JOHN A. HUDSON

Franklin Roosevelt's critics saw his New Deal as nothing more than a chaotic hodgepodge of experiments and contradictions that created more in the way of confusion than relief from the ailments of the Great Depression. Conservative critics charged that Roosevelt's policies ran counter to traditional American capitalism, while radical critics argued that Roosevelt's relief efforts blunted, but did not truly remedy, the injustices that the capitalist system perpetrated on the masses. In the following essay, author and University of Texas scholar George Wolfskill and University of Texas librarian John A. Hudson argue that the experimental nature of the New Deal did not betray a lack of direction. With his New Deal, Roosevelt was striving to find a middle way between laissez-faire economics and socialism. The president sought to save American capitalism, but also to purge it of the "obscenities of Big Business" and create a more humane system.

———————

I N THE EARLY YEARS OF THE DEPRESSION A COMMON EXPERI-ence united the nation. It was not the kind of unity which comes in the wake of some great calamity, some natural disaster which strikes suddenly and is over quickly. Nor was it the kind of unity which defeat by a foreign foe brings—the humiliation of surrender, the rape of national honor, silent tears.

———————

This was a unity of erosion, an erosion of intangibles, of will, of pride, of self-respect, of confidence, the slow, insidious erosion of alert minds, skilled hands, trained muscles. It was an erosion measured in the melting away of life savings, in the foreclosing of mortgages, in searching for cheaper lodging, selling precious household belongings and family heirlooms, in borrowing and stretching credit to the breaking point, in pawning wedding rings and watches, in moving in with relatives, in peddling apples on downtown street corners, in "No Help Wanted" signs, in the shame, the unbearable shame, of honest men asking for relief. From it all emerged a unity of a people, uncommonly patient, numbly asking themselves if there was no end to it; if there was nowhere to turn for a people long stricken.

The Early Days of Roosevelt's Presidency

It was little wonder that no President ever came to the office with greater opportunities or amid so great an outpouring of popular support and trust as Franklin Roosevelt did. There were, of course, some who had misgivings. Walter Lippmann had spoken of Roosevelt as "an amiable man with . . . philanthropic impulses . . . without any important qualifications. . . ." Paul Blanshard, a practicing Socialist in those days, asserted that if Roosevelt were no better President than he was a governor the country "will be preyed upon as it was in the days of Harding." And there were others. But the gainsayers were ignored or quickly forgotten in the early, exciting, electrifying days of the New Deal, days filled with drama and at least the illusion of action, days of smiling reassurance and words of cheer. Of a sudden, it was great again to be alive. . . .

Overwhelming approval and a willingness to give Roosevelt a chance was enough to silence all but the most pessimistic, those who were committed to the working of natural economic laws to cure the ills of the country rather than to what seemed the drastic remedies of the New Deal.

Even they were circumspect; like Herbert Hoover, surveying the scene from the thirty-third floor suite of his son in the Waldorf Astoria Towers, telling reporters there was just one thing to do. We must support the President, advised the sad, bone-weary hero of a happier day. . . .

Opposition Mounts

In April, 1935, in a radio address on the public works program, Roosevelt invited criticism. "Feel free to criticize," he had said. It was just as well; criticism had already begun in earnest during the fall and winter of 1934. . . . In August, 1934, the American Liberty League was formed, an articulate spokesman for the conservative business community which was beginning to recover its nerve. In the elections that fall, the Democrats made criticism an issue, an antidote to the Republican campaign in which candidates, fearing to challenge Roosevelt's popularity, tried to separate him from the New Deal. They liked Roosevelt, they said, liked his humanitarianism, his earnest concern for the underdog, his zealous attack against the Depression on all fronts. But they disliked specific parts of the New Deal. The Democrats based the campaign on the simple proposition that Roosevelt was the New Deal; the voter could not accept the one without the other. . . .

In the spring of 1935, Roosevelt picked up the reins, moved off in a new direction, a direction from which retreat would be uncommonly difficult. In the months of inactivity, of near reverie, he was being pushed relentlessly toward a decision not altogether palatable to him. The decision was a philosophical one, a conscious choice to steer a leftward course, seizing the opportunity for reforms and for security that the depression crisis offered. With continual encouragement, recovery would almost take care of itself; but when it came, the propitious moment for crucial reforms and for built-in safeguards for the public against recurrent adversity would be past, gone with the twin by-products of prosperity—apathy and indifference.

Caught in the Middle

Roosevelt's choice was reached amid a growing conservative mood on the one side, one that pressed the private view that recovery was being delayed by too much Administration radicalism, and an ever widening circle of opinion on the other held by those who had been hit hardest by depression and who had profited least by the New Deal recovery measures, who felt that Roosevelt had not gone far enough. Predictably, the choice begat the most extensive program of social and economic legislation ever undertaken in the history of the country. Roosevelt had not foreseen this turn of events. He was dismayed when his initial program, highly dramatic but largely conventional (the First New Deal, some would call it), did not bring the desired results. And he did not come easily to the role of the gay reformer. But this was to be his role until the rush of world events cast him in a new one, that of warrior.

"The United States, feeling much better, is behaving like all convalescents," wrote the widely respected Arthur Krock of *The New York Times* in the spring of 1935. "Its complaints are mounting." Krock was correct; by 1935, the Roosevelt honeymoon was long since over. Over, too, were the preliminary skirmishes and probing actions. Most people had made up their minds what the New Deal was, or, at least, what they thought the New Deal was. Opinions had crystallized. The verdict was in. What remained was the deadly serious business of acting out conviction. . . .

People could find much in the New Deal with which to disagree, honest people who were often not consciously aware that they even had a political philosophy. Their quarrel with the New Deal was on specifics, an honest difference of opinion on individual matters. . . .

It was also easy to understand why people whose knowledge of economics might be no more than making change at the cigar counter were concerned about government deficits, deficits which mounted annually. The over-simplified argument concerning what happened to the man who consistently spent more than he earned made good sense to them, seemed entirely applicable to governments as well. It was an argument that gained plausibility with every example of New Deal waste and prodigality.

Any number of people were disturbed by an agricultural program that required slaughtering pigs, burning wheat, plowing under cotton, pouring kerosene on potatoes, letting fruit rot on the trees. They did not seem to resent a similar policy of scarcity involving business because fixing prices, dividing markets, adjusting wages, cutting production, reducing inventories, waiving anti-trust laws, did not look like quite the same thing. While people were starving in the midst of plenty, both here and abroad, it all seemed wrong; wrong, damn it, whether you were talking about "wrong" in terms of morality or simple error. New Dealers could talk about the policy of scarcity to raise prices and wages, about how the United States had reached some state of middle-age where the power to produce was outrunning the power to consume and the two had to be restored to some equilibrium, quickly, like jerking the adhesive tape from the patient, they could talk and explain until they were blue in the face, and it still did not make it seem right. . . .

Experiments and Contradictions

Observing the New Deal in action could lead one to the conclusion that it was utterly chaotic, a hodgepodge, a political Hungarian goulash of experiments and contradictions and expedient leftovers. A patient, closer examination would show that it was some other, more desirable things as well. It was, for example (if nothing else), a stopgap. A favorite theme of New Deal critics was that recovery would have come about with or without the New Deal, that in the natural and immutable law of things there would have been a natural recovery, that President Hoover was right all along—prosperity was just around the corner.

That may be. In 1937, Senator Millard Tydings, who had his differences with Roosevelt and who was high on the 1938 "purge" list, looked back on those Depression years and conceded that Roosevelt had probably saved the country. Tydings, who was in basic agreement with the "natural recovery" philosophy, reasoned that something very much like the New Deal had been required at the time to case the pain until recovery came. Criticism of the early New Deal measures reminded Tydings of the story about the drowning man. "A voice from the shore calls out to him, 'Don't be frightened. Be patient. In a few hours the tide will go down and you can wade ashore.'" Tydings' concept of the New Deal was that of a life-preserver, something to keep the victim afloat until the tide went out, until recovery came.

Critics could charge that the New Deal was pragmatic, eclectic, experimental, trial-and-error, and they would all be correct. As Hugh Johnson put it in 1937, Roosevelt would go down in history as "the man who started more creations than were ever begun since Genesis—and finished none." Johnson did not mean that, of course; but it was an interesting way of saying that Roosevelt was at least willing to undertake the new and untried, which usually implied that he did not know what he was doing, that he was frantically pushing buttons and pulling levers hoping that something might accidentally start the machinery.

But the experimental spirit of the New Deal did not mean that it had no sense of direction, no ultimate destination. After a year and four months in office, *The New Republic*, in an article entitled, "The Show Is Over," described the disillusionment and discouragement of Roosevelt's more radical supporters in the Administration, men who despaired of the New Deal, men who lamented over Roosevelt's failure to aim for complete nationalization at a dead run. The talk by Rexford Tugwell and others about rolling up their sleeves and making the country over was only talk. They would never get the chance. The evidence was mounting that Roosevelt was no Communist or Socialist, not even radical enough to suit the Radicals.

In the Liberal Center

If Roosevelt's goals for the New Deal were not clearly socialistic neither were they designed to lead the country back to some imaginary golden age, an age of ancient virtues, political quietism, and McKinley-like piety. Few would admit that the system worked none too well even then for the great majority of the American people. Yet so many of the leaders of American business and industry and finance in the 1930's had begun their climb to wealth and power, and sometimes fame, in the late nineteenth century that Social Darwinism was bred in their bones. Their political vision was clouded by nostalgia for what they regarded as the good old days, the American way of life, the system that had made America great. This was the vantage point from which the American Liberty League and its allies viewed the New Deal. The New Deal was never cautious enough for them.

The goal of the New Deal was not socialism, neither was it geared to a return to nineteenth-century conservatism. Nor was it fascism. That the New Deal was assailed from both sides, from conservatives and radicals alike, is a fair indication that Roosevelt stood somewhere in the liberal center. To some this meant that the New Deal was an attempt to democratize industrial and finance capitalism, to see to it that its fruits were more fairly distributed, that its knavery was permanently curbed. It was, as Herbert Agar put it, a program to promote widespread prosperity without the "obscenities of Big Business.". . .

A Break with Tradition

With some critics the conviction that the New Deal was a break with tradition was sincere. Theirs was the concept of history as having run its course; the historical process was as finished and complete as the Great Pyramid. The American Revolution was the mighty groan of a people straining every muscle, every nerve, to shove the apex stone in place. And now it was finished, at last things were as they should be, a handsome thing to be admired and revered through the ages, its excesses and stupidities buried deep inside with the mummified Pharaoh.

Roosevelt and the New Dealers rejected the concept that America was a finished product. The New Deal was, if nothing else, committed to the fact of constant, steady change, the necessity for governmental action to accommodate to those changes, and the continuing need for explaining to the people, in simple, candid terms, what those changes were all about. There was, then, a strong element of relativity about the New Deal, the belief that democracy was a method, a process, that was ever in a state of becoming, not a fulfilled system of economics, or government, or society, reduced to commandments and preserved on stones, writ by the finger of God.

Roosevelt and the New Deal applied to the Constitution something of that same spirit of change, of relativity, of dynamism. It was not that Roosevelt was flagrantly unconcerned about the supreme law of the land, that he rejected constitutional methods, that he deliberately sought to flaunt it, circumvent it, and, when the moon was right, murder it. He recognized, however, that it was capable of many interpretations (at least it always had been in the past). And he did not intend to stand idly by if it meant letting people starve by strict constitutional methods. If honest men, who stood in awe of the inspired Word, could differ, sometimes vehemently, over its meaning, so other men equally honest could dispute the meanings of the Constitution, which, after all, was not Holy Writ. John Franklin Carter, the Unofficial Observer of the New Deal years, was fairly close to the New Deal position when, in his customary humorous forthrightness, he wrote: "The New Dealers have no designs against the Constitution, provided that it retains the elasticity of the original fabric. This elasticity has always been in evidence whenever a Philadelphia lawyer desired to drive a corporate caravan through it, but it has been remarkably rigid whenever the rights of the common men were up for consideration."

Roosevelt's Faith in the American System

Just as the New Deal was committed to change, so was it committed to the proposition that governmental power was not automatically evil. Power and evil were not the same thing; power could be used for good as readily as for evil; power could only be judged in its specific applications. What the New Dealers were getting at was that there could never be in modern society a moratorium on the use of power. Power existed, it was; if it were not held in one place it would be held in another. There could not be a power vacuum. If government refused to exercise its powers, particularly in economic matters, there were those who would exercise it privately, as New Dealers believed had been the case for years. They believed, sincerely and conscientiously, that the default by government in its use of power had produced an economic situation grossly unfair, one in which the American people consistently got the short end of the stick.

Granted, that the New Deal meant changes and modifications in many areas of economics and social reform. Roosevelt broke more precedents than any President in history. He did more building, more tearing down, and more remodeling than any other President. Yet none, perhaps, believed more firmly in the essential soundness of the American system than Roosevelt. No one was more bitterly disappointed in him than the radicals on each end of the political spectrum. As Frank Kent of the Baltimore *Sun*, a bitter critic of the New Deal, was willing to concede,

Franklin Roosevelt had done "more than any other President to preserve our institutions and stem the tide of both Socialism and Fascism in this country." At the other extreme of political persuasion, Roosevelt was welcomed at first as the executioner of capitalism. But the executioner's axe turned out to be a surgeon's scalpel. The patient returned to robust health. . . .

A Pragmatic Choice

Despite what often looked like a vendetta with business, industrial capitalism and the free enterprise system were never really in any danger from the New Deal. From the first, Roosevelt expected to save the system, to cure its malaise. But he did not intend to do so because private business was somehow sacred. His was a pragmatic choice, not a theological one; a choice that was based on experience, not a divine admonition that had been handed down from on high on a pillar of fire. A system of private business, if it were conducted properly, was the best system in America to serve the public interest. Roosevelt was convinced of that. But business could no longer do as it pleased and call it free enterprise. The New Deal, he told the country, "will not restore that ancient order."

New Deal convictions toward business and the economic policies undertaken were based on a number of serious assumptions. Roosevelt, early in the game, discarded the proposition that the economy moved in mysterious cycles of boom and bust, governed by immutable laws that mere mortals could not comprehend. "No government," Hoover had declared categorically in 1936, "can legislate away the morning after any more than it can legislate away the effects of a tornado—not even the New Deal." The "morning after" was the inevitable hangover from a prosperity spree, as inevitable and irresistible as a tornado.

Roosevelt refused to accept the assumption—and the spirit of resignation to a blind destiny implied in it—that the economic system was some whimsical, capricious, unpredictable thing that could bring pleasure or pain as it wished, and that there was nothing anybody could do about it. The conflict here was between those who believed that operation of the economic system had to be automatic, that it was some kind of perpetual motion machine, and those who put their trust in legislation to regulate and to assist the functioning of the system.

This New Deal commitment led to the conclusion that by wise planning and precautions prosperity was a happy state that could be created and depression avoided. Planning, as in the case of the National Industrial Recovery Act [NIRA] and the Agricultural Adjustment Act [AAA], was one of the prime excuses for charges of dictatorship, of conflicting claims of fascism and socialism leveled at the New Deal. As an aside, it did little good to point out to critics that at the outset businessmen and farm leaders had favored such planning, that the NIRA and AAA were largely designed by businessmen and farmers to save themselves, not by New Dealers. . . .

The Needs of the People

One of the striking characteristics of the New Deal was its humanitarianism, its enthusiastic response to the needs of people, those people so well described by Gerald Johnson in *Incredible Tale* as "people who were not fighters at all, who didn't know how to fight—babies, and small children, charwomen and cooks and housewives in remote places and practitioners of the gentle arts, music, painting, sculpture, the dance. The government was always giving a break to people no one had ever thought of helping before, Negro singers, aspiring playwrights, blind people, all of the dispossessed and disinherited. . . ." And if to the list he added farmers, laborers, old people, and students, it would change nothing. To help them did not mean to ruin others in some devilish geometric progression. . . .

It is true, of course, that most Americans understood and profited by some of the objectives of the New Deal. America was all the better for a social and ethnic revolution which for the first time revised upward the status of great groups of the "forgotten men" in American society, provided them with unprecedented opportunity for escaping a dull and humdrum existence, offered them fulfilment. America was a better place because Roosevelt succeeded in making security for the individual something more than an idle wish; it became an attainable dream, an acceptable part of American political philosophy. America was better off because the New Deal had championed the right of others besides businessmen to participate in decision-making, particularly those decisions affecting economic policy.

But most Americans, friends or foes of Roosevelt, missed the real point of the New Deal. Certainly the critics did. Roosevelt refused to accept the narrow economic determinism implied in both socialism (whether it be of the Marxist variety or whatever) and laissez-faire with its mystical faith in immutable economic laws. Roosevelt rejected the economic fatalism of the arrogant rugged individualist and the doctrinaire collectivist. He was convinced there must be some other way, a middle way. A modified capitalism, a mixed economy was possible, he believed. And he caught hell from both sides for believing it. Once convinced that he was right, that there was a middle way, Roosevelt burned bridges all over the place. What began to emerge from the New Deal experiment was a society that had divorced itself from laissez-faire but which refused to marry socialism. But this was as far as Roosevelt got. He was never able to apply the philosophy of the middle way to anything more than the symptoms of the Depression. The crucial problems of the twentieth century, the problems which had caused the disaster in the first place, were not confronted; they remained unsolved.

People Wanted Action

The most serious problem confronting the country, challenging the minds of statesman and theoretician alike, straining the fabric of the Constitution and the federal system to the breaking point, was how to reconcile traditional freedom for the individual (the freedom of an individual in an agrarian society which the country had inherited from the nineteenth century) with the challenge of industrialization, centralization, monopoly, the maldistribution of wealth, urbanization, of science and automation and technology, all of those things which threatened, which undermined the American dream. . . .

It was the prime domestic question of the twentieth century, and Roosevelt faced it in a time of economic disaster when the country was in no mood to listen to solutions that might right the country in some indefinite long-run. People wanted action, they wanted it quick, and they wanted results. There was no time for seeking a middle way by careful probing, by judicious weighing, by intelligent and selective trial-and-error. The critics did not believe there was a middle way. It was the crowning irony of New Deal criticism that the classical liberal and the Marxist could meet on common ground and solemnly agree that the middle way was impossible, suicidally impossible; for both, the middle way consigned America to a life of economic sin or worse. The pressure for quick results and the dead weight of all-or-nothing, either-or obstructionism meant the New Deal could never be much more than a grand postponement.

The night of Roosevelt's death, Samuel Grafton, the syndicated columnist of the *New York Post*, wrote an obituary. Grafton may have had deeper insight into the New Deal dilemma than any critic or apologist, then or later, when he wrote:

> Leaf-raking was silly. You cannot tell me he did not

know it was silly. He knew. But as against a concentration camp, it was noble. As against what happened in Spain, leaf-raking even had grandeur. I think he knew these things, and there was a knowledge of them in his smile when he was attacked and baited.

He had no answers that were good for a hundred years. But in a six-month crisis he always had a six-month answer. . . . Maybe he had a right to smile, and to think that a billion was not so much; maybe he knew what he had got for it, and that it was a bargain.

Under the circumstances, a six-month answer for a six-month crisis would have to do. Stall for time. Trade dollars for time. Time. Time for the country to collect its wits. Time for the people to pull themselves together, shake their fears, recover their sense of humor, take heart. Time so that America would not default to madmen and lunatics and their wicked dreams. Time so that honest men could find solid answers to pressing problems that the country had been ignoring and fending off for years. Time to vindicate Roosevelt's dream of the middle way. He had seen America through a great agony. Democracy had survived its severest test; it was to have a second chance. As Grafton said, the New Deal was a bargain; Roosevelt did have a right to smile.

CHAPTER
2

THE COURT
PACKING PLAN

Court Reform: Victory in Spite of Defeat

William E. Leuchtenburg

In the early days of Franklin Roosevelt's presidency most of his New Deal legislation encountered little or no opposition. By 1935, however, the Supreme Court, dominated by a bloc of conservative justices, began to overturn key components of the New Deal. Frustrated by the lack of judicial cooperation, Roosevelt planned to inject the Supreme Court with a more liberal element by adding six justices. In the following essay, noted depression-era scholar William E. Leuchtenburg describes how the Court frustrated Roosevelt once again by reversing itself and ruling in favor of many New Deal measures. In the minds of many senators and congressmen, as well as those in the general public, this judicial about-face eliminated the need to alter the composition of the Court. As a result of the Court's reversal, Roosevelt suffered his first major political defeat as president and his judicial reorganization plan was scrapped. Despite this defeat, however, Roosevelt obtained what he set out to win— Supreme Court approval of the New Deal.

FRANKLIN ROOSEVELT'S PROPOSAL TO PACK THE SUPREME Court in 1937 bore the mark of a proud sovereign who after suffering many provocations had just received a new confirmation of power. In November 1936, the President had won the biggest electoral victory in the annals of the two-party system, but his sense of triumph was flawed

Excerpted from *The Supreme Court Reborn: The Constitutional Revolution in the Age of Roosevelt*, by William E. Leuchtenburg. Copyright ©1996 by William E. Leuchtenburg. Used by permission of Oxford University Press, Inc.

by the realization that it was incomplete. Even though he controlled the Executive office and could expect to have his way with Congress, where he had led his party to a smashing victory, the third branch, the Supreme Court, seemed intractable. Four of the Justices—James McReynolds, Pierce Butler, Willis Van Devanter, and George Sutherland—were such staunch conservatives that almost every time either the Solicitor General, Stanley Reed, or the Attorney General, Homer S. Cummings, went into court, he knew he had four votes against him; if he lost even one of the remaining five, he would be beaten. Three judges—Louis Brandeis, Harlan Fiske Stone, and Benjamin Cardozo—would approve most of the New Deal laws. But if either of the two Justices in the center—Chief Justice Charles Evans Hughes or Owen Roberts—moved into the camp of the "Four Horsemen," FDR's program would perish in the courtroom.

Early in the New Deal, the Supreme Court had appeared willing to uphold novel legislation, but in the spring of 1935 the roof had fallen in. Justice Roberts joined the Four Horsemen to invalidate a rail pension law, and thereafter Roberts voted consistently with the conservatives. Later that same month, on "Black Monday," May 27, 1935, the Court, this time in a unanimous decision, demolished the National Industrial Recovery Act. In the next year, the Court, by a 6–3 vote in [*United States v.*] *Butler*, struck down the Agricultural Adjustment Act with an opinion by Justice Roberts that provoked a blistering dissent from Justice Stone; took special pains to knock out the Guffey Coal Act in the *Carter* [*v. Carter Coal Company*] case; and in [*Morehead v. New York ex rel.*] *Tipaldo* invalidated a New York State minimum wage law. "Never in a single year before or since," Max Lerner later wrote, "has so much crucial legislation been undone, so much declared public policy nullified." Of all the wounds the Court inflicted on itself, the *Tipaldo* decision cut deepest. It appeared to create, as Roosevelt said, a "no-man's-land," in which neither the federal government nor any state government could act to protect the worker.

The President Drops a Bombshell

The President said nothing more about the Court publicly for all the rest of 1936, and after his great victory in November he went off on a cruise to South America without intimation that he had any notion of taking action affecting the Court in his second term. In January he gave his inaugural address without indicating that he had any particular plans. The new Congress convened, and more days passed, and still he did not let on what he intended. Then, abruptly, without warning, the President, on February 5, 1937, dropped a bombshell. Instead of calling for new social legislation, he caught the nation, his Congressional leaders, and his closest friends by surprise with a bold, quite unexpected proposal—to alter the composition of the United States Supreme Court.

Roosevelt sent his scheme for reorganizing the judiciary up to the Hill in a special message. He claimed that insufficient personnel had resulted in overcrowded federal court dockets and had occasioned great delay and expense to litigants. "A part of the problem of obtaining a sufficient number of judges to dispose of cases is the capacity of the judges themselves," he stated. "This brings forward the question of aged or infirm judges—a subject of delicacy and yet one which requires frank discussion." He continued:

> In exceptional cases, of course, judges, like other men, retain to an advanced age full mental and physical vigor. Those not so fortunate are often unable to perceive their own infirmities. . . .
>
> A lower mental or physical vigor leads men to avoid an examination of complicated and changed conditions. Little by little, new facts become blurred through old glasses fitted, as it were, for the needs of another gener-

ation; older men, assuming that the scene is the same as it was in the past, cease to explore or inquire into the present or the future.

Life tenure for judges, the President declared, "was not intended to create a static judiciary. A constant and systematic addition of younger blood will vitalize the courts."

To achieve this end, he recommended that when a federal judge who had served at least ten years waited more than six months after his seventieth birthday to resign or retire, a President might add a new judge to the bench. He could appoint as many as six new Justices to the Supreme Court and forty-four new judges to the lower federal tribunals. Even though it was conceivable that if the legislation was enacted, the superannuated Justices, sensing a national will, would choose to resign, thereby leaving the bench at nine members, the plan was perceived to be an attempt to enlarge the Court.

The Response

FDR's message generated an intensity of response unmatched by any legislative controversy of this century, save perhaps for the League of Nations episode. "No issue since the Civil War has so deeply split families, friends, and fellow lawyers," wrote one columnist. Day after day for the next half-year, stories about the Supreme Court conflict rated banner headlines. One diarist noted: "Roosevelt's alteration plan of Supreme Court stirs America. Addresses, talks, arguments for and against it, everywhere." The question was debated at town meetings in New England, at crossroads country stores in North Carolina, at a large rally at the Tulsa courthouse, by the Chatterbox Club of Rochester, New York, the Thursday Study Club of La Crosse, Wisconsin, the Veteran Fire Fighters' Association of New Orleans, and the Baptist Young People's Union of Lime Rock, Rhode Island. In Beaumont, Texas, a movie audience broke out in applause for rival arguments on the plan when they were shown on the screen. . . .

In the first week, numbers of Democratic Senators announced themselves for the bill, including a phalanx of influential legislators: the forceful Majority Leader Joseph T. Robinson of Arkansas; the chairman of the Judiciary Committee, Henry Fountain Ashurst of Arizona, though he disliked it; and such potent allies as Pat Harrison of Mississippi, James F. Byrnes, Jr., of South Carolina, and Key Pittman of Nevada. Men of rather conservative disposition, they received the plan with varying degrees of unenthusiasm but supported it out of loyalty to the President and the Democratic party. More ardent backing came from New Deal liberals such as Hugo Black of Alabama and Sherman Minton of Indiana, both future Supreme Court Justices. After assessing the situation, the White House concluded that no more than fifteen Democrats would oppose the bill in the Senate, and *Time* reported: "Newshawks who immediately made surveys of Congressional sentiment agreed that the bill would be passed without serious difficulty."

Supporters of Court Reform

Greeted in the press with anguished cries of outrage, the plan also elicited no little approbation, especially from FDR's admirers. They argued that the proposal was designed not to pack the Court but to "unpack" it, since the Court had been "stuffed" with corporation lawyers in previous Republican regimes. The whole machinery of American government, they asserted, lay at the will of a single Justice, Owen Roberts, who, by combining with the Four Horsemen, could nullify the wishes of the people. A number of the bill's proponents charged that the Court had usurped its powers; some even denied that there was any constitutional sanction for judicial review. Moreover, they found ample historical precedent for altering the size of

Judicial Supremacy Is Unconstitutional

Senator Robert M. La Follette of Wisconsin was a supporter of judicial reorganization. In the following excerpt from a speech given on February 13, 1937, La Follette describes the need to check building judicial supremacy in American government.

Article I of the Constitution specifically provides that "all legislative powers herein granted shall be vested in the Congress of the United States." The Founding Fathers never dreamed that legislative policies adopted by the Congress in carrying out powers clearly delegated to it were to be subject to a rigid judicial review amounting to a judicial veto. Proposals to give the Supreme Court even a limited veto power over legislation were rejected by an overwhelming vote in the Constitutional Convention. . . .

The idea of an unchecked supremacy of the Supreme Court has been built up only over the last forty years. It

the bench. Nor would they concede that Roosevelt was politicizing the Court; Representative Thomas R. Amlie, a Wisconsin Progressive, contended: "The fact is that the Supreme Court has always been in politics up to its ears.". . .

Supporters of the plan scoffed at the reverent attitude opponents took toward the Constitution and the Court. "A constitution is not an idol to be worshipped; it is an instrument of government to be worked," maintained Senator Robert J. Bulkley of Ohio. Many doubted the sincerity of the Constitution-worshippers. A South Carolinian observed: "If I got up tomorrow and advocated rigid adherence to the 14th and 15th [Amendments] of the Constitution, the same folks who are yelling 'Constitution' loudly has been built up by corporation lawyers of the Liberty League [a conservative organization] ilk who have tried in the Court to counteract the reforms, like popular election of Senators, which are designed to make the will of the people the law of the land. It has been indoctrinated in our schools and in our thinking with the same conscious direction as the propaganda of the public utilities. If the Congress continues to acquiesce in such a pernicious doctrine, the Congress will be guilty of abandoning its constitutional rights and duties. The Constitution provides for a separation of powers, not for a judicial supremacy. The idea of judicial supremacy is not found in the Constitution or the writings of the Constitutional fathers. It is an idea of smart lawyers who, beaten in the Congress, have sought for their own advantage to twist and distort the Constitution ever since its adoption.

Congressional Speech, available at www.newdeal.feri.org/cong/ congress001.htm.

now would fight among themselves for priority in applying the tar and feathers." Henry M. Hart of the Harvard Law School contested the notion that a Supreme Court opinion was like the pronouncement of a Delphic oracle, and Donald Richberg, former chairman of the National Industrial Recovery Board, asserted: "We need to be disillusioned of the idea that putting a black robe upon a man makes him a superior variety of human being." . . .

The Opposition

Although such sentiments strengthened the hand of the Administration Democrats in the Senate, the bill also encountered vigorous opposition, far more than had been anticipated. Roosevelt must have expected the defection of anti–New Deal Democrats such as Carter Glass of Virginia and Josiah Bailey of North Carolina. Much more serious was the rebellion of party regulars like Tom Connally of Texas and of the liberal Democrat Burton K. Wheeler of Montana. The loss of Wheeler was a stunner. After all, in 1924 Wheeler had been the vice-presidential nominee on the Progressive ticket headed by Robert M. La Follette, Sr., who charged the federal judiciary with usurpation and wanted to authorize Congress to override Supreme Court rulings. Since no one could dispute his credentials as a liberal, Wheeler, by denouncing the plan, made it difficult for the President to claim that his adversaries were the same bunch of economic royalists who had fought him in 1936. . . .

The strategy of the crowded dockets–advanced age rationale turned out to be a blunder, and in March, the President virtually abandoned that line of argument and came out with his primary reason: that the Court was dominated by conservative Justices who were making it impossible for a national government to function. This emphasis appealed to FDR's New Deal followers, but others bristled at any attempt to tamper with an institution established by the Founding Fathers. Although the number of Justices had been changed several times before, many believed that the Constitution specified nine. One writer encountered an elderly lady who protested, "If nine judges were enough for George Washington, they should be enough for President Roosevelt. I don't see why he needs fifteen." In vain, supporters of the bill retorted that the Founding Fathers had been revolutionaries and that the opponents were attempting to escape modern problems by evoking nostalgia for a mythical past. . . .

A Shift in the Court

The Court itself, however, had some big surprises in store. On March 29, by 5–4 in the [*West Coast Hotel v.*] *Parrish* case with Justice Roberts joining the majority, the Court upheld a minimum wage statute from the state of Washington that to most people seemed identical to the New York law it had wiped out in *Tipaldo* less than a year before. Two weeks later, Roberts joined in a series of 5–4 decisions finding the National Labor Relations Act constitutional. On May 24, the Court validated the Social Security law. These rulings marked a historic change in constitutional doctrine. The Court was now stating that local and national governments had a whole range of powers that this same tribunal had been saying for the past two years these governments did not have.

The crucial development was the switch of Justice Roberts, which converted a 5–4 division against New Deal legislation to 5–4 in favor. Some have argued that Roberts did not change at all. They explain that his vote against the New York minimum wage law in *Tipaldo* resulted from his unwillingness to rule on questions not properly brought before the Court, a contention that is unpersuasive. More important, if the Social Security opinions are contrasted to the *Rail Pension* ruling and to *Butler,* and the Wagner Act opinions are set against the *Carter* decision, it is clear that the Court, and specifically Mr. Justice Roberts, had shifted ground. . . .

This argument became even more compelling when on the morning of May 18, while the President was breakfasting in bed, a messenger arrived at the White House with a letter from one of the Four Horsemen, Justice Willis Van Devanter, announcing his resignation from the bench. Van Devanter's action was widely believed to have been the result of counsel from Senators Borah and Wheeler. Borah lived in the same apartment house on Connecticut Avenue; the two were on "Hello, Bill" and "Hello, Willis" terms. The "conversion" of Roberts had given Roosevelt a 5–4 majority; soon he would be able to name someone to take Van Devanter's place and have the opportunity for a 6–3 advantage.

Roosevelt Pursues Reorganization

Since it appeared that the President had won substantially what he sought, he was now urged to call off the fight. "Why," it was asked, "shoot the bridegroom after a shotgun wedding?" The *Parrish* and Wagner Act decisions turned some Senators against the plan and encouraged others to press for compromise. Prentiss Brown stated that the switch of the Court took "a good deal of the ground work from under the arguments for the court bill and I believe it will open the way for friends and opponents to re-approach the issue." By the end of April, the two sides were roughly even. One poll showed forty-four Senators in favor, forty-seven opposed, four doubtful, with one seat vacant. The Social Security opinions and Van Devanter's resignation tipped the balance against the six-judge bill; thereafter, opponents held a narrow edge.

Several in the FDR circle wanted to drop the whole project, but others argued that Justices who could switch so easily in his favor could just as easily jump back once the pressure was off. One of the President's aides said: "No man's land now is Roberts land." The Scripps Howard columnist Raymond Clapper noted in his diary that Roosevelt's press secretary had told him "that president is going ahead with fight—that don't know how long Hughes can keep Roberts liberal or how long Hughes will stay so." Others reasoned that the switch of the Court had proven what the President had been saying all along: there was nothing wrong with the Constitution, only with the Court. And if enlightenment was such a good thing, why not have more of it? Senator Theodore Green of Rhode Island declared: "Again we learn that the Constitution is what Mr. Justice Roberts says it is. So what we need is not amendments to the Constitution, but a sufficient number of judges to construe it broadly, lest one man's mistaken opinion may decide the fate of a nation."

"Why Compromise?"

Furthermore, Roosevelt believed the country was with him. Only half a year had gone by since his decisive victory at the polls. "Why compromise?" the Democratic party chairman, Jim Farley, asked. "The Democratic senators were elected on the basis of supporting the President's program. It is up to them to back it now." To be sure, mail ran heavily against the bill, but since attitudes toward the plan divided sharply on class lines, and upper income groups were more articulate, that was not surprising. Members of Congress noted that opponents of the proposal often wrote on lithographed and embossed stationery, and when they analyzed their mail, they frequently found, too, that adverse letters came overwhelmingly from Republicans who in the recent campaign had been noisy but outnumbered. If the press denounced the plan, 80 percent of editorial writers had been against FDR in 1936, and look what had happened on Election Day. True, by now the polls also showed a small margin unfavorable to the bill, but remember how wrong the *Literary Digest* canvass had been a few months before. Only one significant election had been held since the President sent his message, and in that race a Congressional seat in Texas had been won by a candidate committed to the plan, a newcomer named Lyndon B. Johnson. . . .

Well before the end of May, however, FDR's lieutenants in Congress had to face up to the fact that they simply did not have the votes. One leader confided that five polls of the Senate had all come out with the same result: defeat. . . .

Defeat

On July 22, the Senate unceremoniously returned the legislation to committee, from which it never emerged. The President and his supporters could claim that Congress never actually voted down the measure, but no amount of obfuscation could disguise the reality: Roosevelt had suffered a severe setback, and his proposal had drawn its last breath. The Court-packing scheme, declared a Mississippi paper, was as "dead as a salt mackerel shining beneath the pale moonlight," and, as if that were not final enough, added, "as dead as the ashes of Moses, world's first law giver." "The Senate today 're-committed' the ill advised and dangerous bill to 'pack' the U. S. Supreme Court," a Colorado Congressman wrote in his diary. "*Requiescat in pace.*"

The "Roosevelt Court"

But for FDR, all was not lost. Not only did he have a Court that was ruling in favor of the constitutionality of New Deal laws, but also he had the right to appoint someone to the Van Devanter vacancy. Moreover, in astonishing contrast to his experience in his first term, other opportunities rapidly came his way. Within two and a half years after the defeat of the Court proposal, the President was able to choose five of the nine Justices, including his Solicitor General, Stanley Reed, and his adviser, Felix Frankfurter. Indeed, as one historian has pointed out, in less than four years after the end of the legislative struggle, Roosevelt "had named more Justices than any President since George Washington." Before he was done, he had filled eight vacancies and had elevated Harlan Fiske Stone to the Chief Justiceship. "Roosevelt," another historian has written, "succeeded more than any other President in packing the court."

This new Court—the "Roosevelt Court" as it was called—ruled favorably on every one of the New Deal laws whose constitutionality was challenged. It expanded the commerce power and the taxing and spending power so greatly that it soon became evident that there was almost no statute for social welfare or the regulation of business that the Court would not validate. Though the Court had once held that the national government lacked power over even major industries, because, it said, those industries were not in interstate commerce, the Court now permitted Washington to reach into the most remote enterprises. In one case, it ruled that a farmer was engaged in interstate commerce even when he grew wheat wholly for his own consumption on his own farm.

Since 1937 the Court has not struck down a single piece of Congressional legislation constraining business. Although before 1937 legal realism influenced only a few Justices, thereafter the old doctrines of constitutional fundamentalism lost out. Whereas the beneficiaries of the Court before 1937 had been businessmen and other propertied interests, after 1937 they became less advantaged groups. As early as the first week of June 1937, *Business Week* was complaining: "The cold fact is that, for all practical purposes, the reorganization of the Court, sought by legislative process, has been accomplished by the ordinary process of court decision." Eight months later, Frank Gannett wrote: "Since the President now controls the Supreme Court, our only hope lies in influencing the members of Congress."

Early in 1940, a holding company attorney, Wendell Willkie, who later that year would be FDR's opponent in the presidential contest, wrote resignedly:

> Mr. Roosevelt has won. The court is now his. . . . Mr. Roosevelt has accomplished exactly what he would have accomplished if he had won the court fight. . . . When a series of reinterpretations overturning well-argued precedents are made in a brief time by a newly appointed group of Judges, all tending to indicate the same basic disagreement with the established conception of government, the thoughtful observer can only conclude that something revolutionary is going on. And that is what has happened here.
>
> During the past three years the American people have had a series of majority opinions from the Supreme

Court that substantially change their form of government. On almost every occasion on which the court has
been called upon to decide, it has wiped out state and
local lines, and has relentlessly extended Federal authority to every farm, every hamlet, every business firm
and manufacturing plant in the country.

THE COURT PACKING PLAN DAMAGED ROOSEVELT'S REPUTATION

JOHN A. WOODS

Though Roosevelt's attempt to reorganize the Supreme Court eventually led to Court approval of the New Deal, author John A. Woods writes that it had many negative repercussions. Roosevelt's bid to intimidate Congress into passing the Court bill cost him the support and cooperation of his own Democratic Party as well as the Congress as a whole. The embarrassing defeat of the Court Plan, the first such defeat during Roosevelt's tenure as president, also dispelled the myth of Roosevelt's invincibility and set the tone for future defeats for the president in Congress.

T HE NINE JUSTICES OF THE SUPREME COURT, APPOINTED BY the President with the approval of the Senate and holding office for life, make the final decision on the constitutionality of both federal and state legislation. When a majority of them decides that a law is in conflict with the provisions of the Constitution, it ceases to be valid. Like other courts, the Supreme Court strives to follow the precedents established by previous cases, but it is not rigidly bound by them. It has, moreover, developed in the course of time such a variety of principles of constitutional law that a distinguished commentator was led to conclude in 1934 that "the Supreme Court is vested with substantially complete freedom of choice whether to sustain

Excerpted from *Roosevelt and Modern America*, by John A. Woods (London: English Universities Press, 1959). Copyright ©1959 by John A. Woods.

or to overturn the New Deal."

The Supreme Court, as we have seen, decided against a number of important parts of the New Deal. Before 1860 it had made only two decisions against federal enactments; between 1860 and 1920 thirty-nine; and between 1920 and 1930 nineteen. In the three years after 1933 it rendered twelve decisions against the Federal Government, while at the same time it overthrew important state legislation. . . .

A Republican Court

Roosevelt had long been aware of the damage which the Supreme Court might inflict on his programme. During the 1932 campaign he had referred to the fact that from 1929 onwards the Republican Party had been in complete control of the national government: "The Executive, the Senate, the House of Representatives and, I might add for good measure, the Supreme Court as well." President Hoover had promptly rebuked him for his irreverence. It is worth noting that the reference to the Court was a departure from his carefully prepared text. Roosevelt naturally did not take kindly to the havoc which the Court created. He described the decision against the National Recovery Administration to a press conference as a return to the "horse and buggy definition of interstate commerce", and defined the issue raised by the Court in broad terms: "Is the United States going to decide, are the people of this country going to decide, that their Federal Government shall in future have no rights under any implied power or any court-approved power to enter into a solution of a national economic problem, but that the national economic problem must be decided only by the states?" He pointed out the impossibility of solving a national problem through forty-eight legislatures. . . .

The President was not alone in desiring to curb the power of the Court. Three plans had met with substantial support. One would have given power to Congress to overrule the Court. Another would have insisted that two-thirds of the justices must believe an Act to be unconstitutional before it could be declared void. A third would have given Congress by amendment explicit power to regulate industry and agriculture. Legislation which attempted to control the activities of the Court was itself, of course, likely to be declared unconstitutional. The difficulties in obtaining an amendment were also recognized to be very great. It requires favourable action by three-quarters of the states to ratify an amendment. In terms of population, therefore, a very small percentage of the people could prevent its being adopted. An amendment can be easily defeated, for the battle is a dispersed one. There are great difficulties in framing an amendment; when its language has been agreed upon and it has survived the local struggles over its adoption, even then it is subject to judicial interpretation by the same judges whom many believed were nullifying the plain language of the Constitution.

A Critical Error

The President sent his proposals for judicial reform to Congress on the fifth of February 1937. The argument of the message which embodied them was that the Court was behind on its work. The President referred to the fact that the Court had declined to hear appeals in 717 cases out of the 867 brought by private litigants in the previous fiscal year. "Many of the refusals were doubtless warranted. But can it be said that full justice is achieved when a court is forced by the sheer necessity of keeping up with its business to decline without even an explanation, to hear 87 per cent of the cases presented to it by private litigants?" He attributed this state of affairs in part to the age of the justices. "Modern complexities," he explained, "call also for a constant infusion of new blood in the courts, just as it is needed in executive functions of the government and in private business. A lowered mental or physical vigor leads men to avoid an examination of complicated and changed conditions. Little by little, new facts become blurred through old glasses fitted, as it were, for the needs of another generation; older men, assuming that the scene is the same as it was in the past, cease to explore or inquire into the present or the future." He therefore recommended that for each judge over seventy who did not retire a new judge should be added to the Court, but that the number of the Court should never exceed fifteen. "A constant and systematic addition of young blood will vitalize the courts and better equip them to recognize and apply the essential concepts of justice in the light of the needs and the facts of an ever-changing world."

The President's placing of emphasis upon the age of the judges was a disastrous error, the effects of which it was impossible to undo. Everyone knew that it was the opinions and not the age of the judges which was the real issue, and the President had only skirted that question. Indeed, the stress laid on age inevitably offended [Louis] Brandeis, the oldest of the judges, and the chief liberal on the Court. No one was likely to forget that the great [Oliver Wendell] Holmes had retired in 1932 at the age of ninety-one. The President afterwards admitted that he had made a mistake, and he soon recognized the need to speak his mind. In March therefore in a forthright "fireside" chat he explained his position, but without, of course, effacing the first unfavourable impression. . . .

Defeat

The storms that broke over the President's plan filled the political atmosphere until the essential part of it was abandoned on the twenty-second of July. The President did obtain an important Act; but he was defeated on the proposal to increase the number of Supreme Court justices. He showed gross overconfidence in introducing the plan with no political preparation and with the basic offence of insincerity stamped upon it. But his overconfidence was to some extent matched by the despondency of those who opposed it. Senator [Carter] Glass, who was very hostile to it, remarked with bitterness that Congress would commit suicide if the President so requested. But the real truth is that the plan offered so much violence to an accepted and revered tradition—the independence of the judiciary—that it never stood more than a slight chance of being enacted, and the method of its presentation probably destroyed all prospect of its adoption.

Democrat vs. Democrat

The opposition to the plan was wisely left by the Republicans to the Democrats. A strong attack from political opponents might have caused the majority to close its ranks. It was pleasant for the minority to watch from the sidelines the spectacle of Democrats attacking Democrats. The President had expected the more conservative members of his own party to oppose the plan. He was surprised when they were joined by many who were whole-hearted supporters of the New Deal. Among those who declined to support the plan was Senator George Norris, though he voted for it in the end. There were desertions elsewhere. Governor Herbert Lehman of New York did not approve; neither did Professor Felix Frankfurter, the distinguished jurist whom Roosevelt later appointed to the Court, and who was close to the highest circles of the New Deal. The Administration was determined to fight for the plan, and was never, until the situation was altogether hopeless, prepared to look for a compromise, not even a compromise which would divide the opposition. The rather cynical pressure it put on Senators further exacerbated the feelings of the legislature. . . .

The actions of the Court itself were even more influential. On the twenty-ninth of March in *West Coast Hotel Company v. Parrish*, the Adkins case was overruled. There were four dissents. On the twelfth of April in five separate cases the Wagner Act was upheld. One case was decided unanimously; there were four dissents in each of the others. On the twenty-fourth of May the Social Security Act was upheld in four cases. The unemployment compensation features were found constitutional by five justices; the old age benefits by seven. The Court did not at this time overrule previous decisions—except the Adkins case—but its earlier rebuffs to New Deal legislation furnished the arguments for the new minority. These decisions made, as the Senate Judiciary Committee noted, the "packing" of the Court unnecessary.

The change in the Supreme Court—"the switch in time which saved nine"—is explained by the fact that Justice Roberts joined the Chief Justice, Brandeis, Cardozo and Stone to make a majority. The Chief Justice had once said that the Constitution is what the judges say it is. It was now remarked that the Constitution was what Justice Roberts said it was. An explanation of his change is essential to a judgment on the Supreme Court plan, for if its introduction influenced Roberts then it cannot be regarded as a complete failure. . . .

Justice Van Devanter Retires

A final blow was delivered by the Court when Justice [Willis] Van Devanter announced his intention to retire. An Act had been passed which created favourable financial conditions for judges who retired. In normal circumstances this would have meant that Roosevelt could have ensured the dominance of the liberal *bloc*. It so happened, however, that the President had promised the next vacancy to Senator Joseph Robinson, his loyal leader in the Senate, and Robinson was conservative in his views. The President handled this embarrassment with some cleverness. He explained to Robinson that he would make the nomination, but not until a modified Court plan had been acted upon. Since Robinson's colleagues were sympathetic with his ambitions, the battle could be kept going. When Robinson suddenly collapsed and died, this last motive for continuing the struggle for a reform of the Court disappeared. On the twenty-second of July the plan was abandoned.

The death of Robinson made vacant the leadership of the Democratic Party in the Senate. Roosevelt further worsened his relations with the Senate by supporting undercover the candidature of Senator Alben Barkley while preserving a surface neutrality. Even his first appointment to the Supreme Court created embarrassment, for his nominee, Senator [Hugo] Black, was shown after he had been confirmed to have been a member of the Ku Klux Klan. (His later record in the defence of civil liberties was to be excellent.) Roosevelt had chosen him because the Senate seldom refuses to confirm the nomination of one of its own members to any post, and Black was one of his most vigorous supporters in that body.

A Younger, More Cooperative Court

With the passage of time, the Court came to consist of justices appointed by Roosevelt. It became younger. In 1945, even after Justice Roberts' successor was appointed, the average age was fifty-seven, compared with seventy-two during the battle over court reform. The doctrine of judicial restraint came into its own, and was found to present its special difficulties, particularly in the fields of civil liberties and the relations between the states. The revolution in judicial interpretation had three broad consequences. A greater latitude had been won for the Federal Government. During the rest of Roosevelt's presidency only one federal enactment was declared unconstitutional: a minor provision which was held to infringe the right to a fair trial. A new co-operation between the Federal Government and the states was allowed to rise and flourish, and "due process" ceased to be the great barrier to social reform which it once had been.

What should be the final judgment upon the attempt to change judicial interpretation by increasing the number of judges? Roosevelt himself claimed that he had lost a battle and won a war. He thought it would be "a little naïve" to deny a connection between the proposal to increase the number of judges and the rapid sustaining of important legislation. There can be no question that the views of the Supreme Court would have gradually changed; that would have been the inevitable consequence of new appointments to the Court. All Roosevelt gained was time. The legislation which was upheld and might have been declared void was unquestionably important. Nevertheless, the price paid by Roosevelt for his temerity in challenging the Court was high. His defeat made easier later defeats. It had been conclusively demonstrated that despite great personal popularity, the President could be soundly beaten. He paid a high price also for the embittered feelings which he created in Congress and which formed a sombre background to the important issues in foreign relations which had already arisen. It would be interesting to know with any certainty how the defeat affected the President himself. It is clear that he felt it deeply; but how much it contributed to the over-cautiousness which many felt he occasionally showed in the next few years it is impossible to tell.

Roosevelt's Attempt to Pack the Court Was an Abuse of Power

RAYMOND MOLEY

In addition to the enormous and relatively unchallenged success Franklin Roosevelt enjoyed during his first term as president, his overwhelming victory in the election of 1936 led the president to believe that he alone represented the will of the people. The only obstacle standing in Roosevelt's path at this time was the Supreme Court, which had invalidated key components of his New Deal. In the following essay, Raymond Moley, one of the architects of the New Deal and an opponent of the president's Court Plan, writes how Roosevelt's attempt to browbeat Congress into letting him appoint six additional justices to the Supreme Court exposed his belief in his own infallibility.

T*HE COURT DISAPPROVES*, ROOSEVELT CALLED THE 1935 volume of his collected papers, and the 1936 volume, *The People Approve.*

That no such appeal from the Court to the voters as these titles suggest was made in 1936 is a matter of record. Still these titles afford a significant clue to Roosevelt's psychology. No doubt his firm belief, or rather his firm will to believe, that the people of this country had given him a general cease-and-desist order to execute against all who challenged him led him to his greatest defeat.

The announcement of the plan to pack the Supreme

Excerpted from *After Seven Years: A Political Analysis of the New Deal*, by Raymond Moley (New York: Harper & Bros., 1939). Copyright ©1939 by Raymond Moley.

Court caught wholly off guard a public and a Congress lulled by three months of exquisite calm. Roosevelt's pronouncements in the course of his goodwill trip to South America would not have frightened the birds of St. Francis. His quiet message to Congress asked cooperation from the Supreme Court in a manner to which even the sternest constitutionalist could not object. His second inaugural speech was peaceable and statesmanlike. For the most part, the man-sobered-by-great-victory tableau was accepted without reserve. Only a few lynx-eyed observers pointed to the jokers in the Reorganization message of January 12, 1937. Only a few people who knew the President very well indeed wondered, privately, just how and when the quiet would be shattered this time.

The stunning answer came on February 5th.

A Plan for Supreme Court Approval

The President's bare attempt to pack the Court was not at all concealed by his arguments that the Court needed enlargement because it was inefficient, because age was related to inefficiency, and because age and conservatism went hand in hand. It was recognized at once for what it was— a plan to provide in advance for Supreme Court approval of whatever legislative reforms Roosevelt happened to espouse, a plan to enable Roosevelt to control the Court.

As such, a number of citizens, like myself, were compelled to fight it with all the resources at our command, although we felt no less strongly than the President that the majority of the Court had arbitrarily held too narrow a view of the powers the Constitution confers upon Congress. In editorials, speeches, and in testimony given to the Senate Judiciary Committee, I opposed it as a palpable makeshift that would remove only temporarily the evil it was designed to remedy, as an impairment of those democratic institutions and traditions that make progressive evolution possible, as a fundamental change which the citizens *alone* had the right to authorize. My opposition was open, whole-hearted, complete, despite a suggestion from Tom Corcoran [a presidential adviser] that I'd better not stick my neck out, because my "side" was going to lose anyhow. . . .

Sometime before the end of December a critical decision was made by Roosevelt and [Attorney General Homer S.] Cummings—the decision to dress up a Court-packing scheme as a general reorganization of the federal judiciary, and slip it through as such. This strangely transparent plan of presentation was not solely a Cummings' adaptation of a recommendation made in 1913 by the then Attorney General James Clark McReynolds. It was also the derivative of a suggestion received in a letter from a friend of the President who lived far from Washington. But unquestionably, in finally deciding on the scheme, the President was swayed by the consideration that the plan could partly be traced back to his archenemy on the Court—McReynolds. Such a straining for incidental effects which appeal to his sense of humor or drama was to appear over and over again in Roosevelt's career thereafter. It is clear the President was carried away by his intense desire to be astute. And it was a tangled web he wove in the name of cleverness—a web that ultimately closed around him. . . .

An Assault on Governmental Principles

Whether or not Roosevelt realized that the plan he championed that day was an assault upon a fundamental principle in American government is another question. Certainly Corcoran, to whom he unfolded the complete plan days before he chose to announce it to the congressional leaders, was appalled only by its indirection. Neither Corcoran nor Cummings objected to it as the violation of a constitutional tradition as binding as a written provision of the Constitution. Roosevelt, himself, familiar though he was with the superficies of American history, had never evidenced, in the years of my association with him, any appreciation of the basic philosophic distinctions in the history of American political thought. The simple principle that democracy exists only in so far as its objectives are attained in terms of its own institutions—this is not necessarily known to the connoisseur of historical anecdotes.

But even if it had been, how much of an obstacle would it have been to a man who believed himself the personification of the will of the majority? Passionately convinced, as Roosevelt was, of the essential purity and rectitude of his intentions, how could he have been expected to remember the injunction in the *Federalist*: "Until the people have, by some solemn and authoritative act, annulled or changed the established form, it is binding upon themselves collectively, as well as individually; and no presumption, or even knowledge, of their sentiments can warrant their representatives in a departure from it." Completely assured, as he was, that he himself embodied the desire for progressivism—that he was progressivism—how could he have been expected to consult those men, many of them immediately within reach at the other end of Pennsylvania Avenue, who might have refreshed his memory?

And so came the second tactical blunder in the proceeding—the failure to take counsel with the congressional leaders on the assumption that they would not dare to oppose his wishes. The election had so far erased the picture of the reception of the "soak-the-rich" program in the summer of 1935 that the Court plan was thrown before Congress with even more imperious abruptness.

On the morning of February 5th Roosevelt presented the congressional leaders with his bill, read a few snatches from his message to them and the Cabinet, and rushed out of the meeting into a press conference. That was all. There was no discussion, no request for advice. He was not asking them: he was telling them. The mechanical processes of preparing these documents for transmission to Congress were all but completed. Exactly two hours later the message was being read to Congress. At no point did he seem to doubt that the tried and true leaders of his party would supinely do his bidding. . . .

"Defeatist Lawyers"

When it became apparent that the opposition would not be deflected, that the ranks of the faithful included many who inwardly deplored the scheme, the President was asked to compromise. His private answer was a burst of scornful laughter. His public answer, delivered before thirteen hundred Democrats in the Mayflower on March 4th, was a warning to the members of his party in Congress that ". . . we cannot afford . . . to run away from [the] fight on advice of defeatist lawyers."

"Defeatist" was the response made again and again that spring to all proposals of compromise that were put to Roosevelt, as the noble fight "of all those who truly believe in political and economic democracy" became a protracted process of political bludgeoning. What was euphemistically called "trench warfare" in behalf of the measure ranged from vague threats to last-minute offers of patronage by powerful subordinates. These things, plus the effects of a series of Supreme Court decisions boldly cutting the ground from under the plan's proponents, plus the growing evidence of public abhorrence for the plan, plus the feeling in the Senate that the President should have made it unmistakably clear if he intended to give Joe Robinson the Van Devanter vacancy on the Supreme Court—all were the ingredients of the most elaborate crow pie any American President had eaten for eighteen years.

On June 14th a majority of the Judiciary Committee of the Senate issued the magnificent report that will rank as one of the major state papers in the history of the country.

> We recommend the rejection of this bill as a needless, futile and utterly dangerous abandonment of constitu-

tional principle [it concluded].

It was presented to the Congress in a most intricate form and for reasons that obscured its real purpose.

It would not banish age from the bench nor abolish divided decisions.

It would not affect the power of any court to hold laws unconstitutional nor withdraw from any judge the authority to issue injunctions.

It would not reduce the expense of litigation nor speed the decision of cases.

It is a proposal without precedent or justification.

It would subjugate the courts to the will of Congress and the President and thereby destroy the independence of the judiciary, the only certain shield of individual rights.

It contains the germ of a system of centralized administration of law that would enable an executive so minded to send his judges into every judicial district in the land to sit in judgment on controversies between the government and the citizen.

It points the way to the evasion of the Constitution and establishes the method whereby the people may be deprived of their right to pass upon all amendments of the fundamental law.

It stands now before the country, acknowledged by its proponents as a plan to force judicial interpretation of the Constitution, a proposal that violates every sacred tradition of American democracy.

Under the form of the Constitution it seeks to do that which is unconstitutional.

Its ultimate operation would be to make this government one of men rather than one of law, and its practical operation would be to make the Constitution what the executive or legislative branches say it is—an interpretation to be changed with each change of administration.

It is a measure which should be so emphatically rejected that its parallel will never again be presented to the free representatives of the free people of America.

The Court Bill Dies

On July 20th [Vice President] John Garner solemnly announced to the President that the plan was licked. The bill was officially buried on July 22, 1937.

Before that day every characteristic implicit in Roosevelt's development between May, 1935, and November, 1936, had reached its full flower. There was the snatching at a half-baked scheme which commended itself chiefly because of its disingenuousness. There was the essential carelessness of its preparation. There was the arbitrary secrecy before its launching. There was the indifference to the fact that it was an unjustifiable means to an end. There was the conviction that he epitomized the progressive will, that his New Deal represented the Ultima Thule of progressive reform. There was the assurance of unquestioned mastery. There was the incredibly stubborn refusal to yield when he still might have escaped absolute defeat. There was the ruthless way in which he lashed supporters, like [Senator] Joe Robinson, insisting that they serve him beyond their power to serve with conviction or effectiveness. Finally, in defeat, there were the supreme confidence that "the people are with me" and the bitter determination to exterminate politically all who had committed the treason of disagreement.

CHAPTER

3

AMERICAN
INTERVENTION IN
WORLD WAR II

THE LEND-LEASE ACT PREPARED AMERICAN INDUSTRY FOR WAR

LEONARD BAKER

When World War II started in 1939, it quickly became apparent that England and France would require American assistance to defeat Nazi Germany. Arguing that England was America's first line of defense against Nazi aggression, President Roosevelt pushed the Lend-Lease Act through Congress. In addition to allowing Roosevelt to circumvent America's Neutrality Acts and provide vital aid to England and France, notes historian Leonard Baker, the Lend-Lease Act served another important purpose. The large amounts of weaponry and machinery provided to the Allied armies through the Lend-Lease Act prepared American industry for the day the United States entered the war as a combatant. When America was forced to enter the war, American industry was already operating at wartime production levels and was able to supply American armed forces with the weapons and machinery needed for victory.

THE MORNING OF SUNDAY, MARCH 9, 1941, WINSTON Churchill awoke at his country estate Chequers to find his secretary waiting with a message. Harry Hopkins [one of Roosevelt's advisers] had called from Washington during the night while the Prime Minister was sleeping. Churchill heard Hopkins' message and then quickly sent him a reply.

Excerpted from *Roosevelt and Pearl Harbor*, by Leonard Baker (New York: Macmillan, 1970). Copyright ©1970 by Leonard Baker. Reprinted by permission of the Estate of Leonard Baker.

"Thank God for your news," said the Churchill answer to Hopkins. "The strain is serious."

The news telephoned across the Atlantic by Hopkins was that the Senate had approved the lend-lease program. Churchill was to later describe this program as the most unsordid act in all of human history.

When [Admiral] William Leahy [chief of naval operations] heard the news in Vichy France, he thought, "This definitely puts the United States in a position from which it must, for its own security, take any action that is necessary to insure the success of Great Britain in the present war."

Both estimates were correct.

The lend-lease program committed the United States to becoming the arsenal of democracy. The United States would manufacture the weapons of war while the English would fight the Germans with those weapons.

The Need for American Assistance

The British need for American assistance had been apparent as soon as the war had begun in 1939. "There is no question that the war is going to be conducted with eyes constantly on the United States," [Ambassador] Joe Kennedy had reported to the President from the American embassy in London when the war was only one week old. "Unless the war comes to a standstill and it is a stalemate between the Germans and the French on the Maginot and Siegfried lines, the English are going to think of every way of maintaining favorable public opinion in the United States, figuring that sooner or later they can obtain real help from America."

During the First World War, when they were fighting together, England and the United States had cooperated on military matters. This concept of cooperation had faded after that war. In 1938, however, the two nations agreed to offer each other's fleet assistance in case both nations were involved in a war with Japan. The agreement, although a loose one, did reestablish the concept of military cooperation between the two nations.

In November, 1939, as a second step in reviving the concept of military cooperation, FDR had persuaded Congress to amend the neutrality laws so that England and France could buy weapons of war on a "cash and carry" basis. Not only had FDR approved of the sales then but he had also established a policy of making a large part of America's military production available for sale in England.

The Equipment Shortage

By the time of the battle of Dunkirk in 1940, when Britain rescued its army from the European continent, the concept of cooperation between England and the United States had not yet evolved enough in detail to have much meaning. George Marshall [chief of staff] has best summed up the situation the British and the Americans were then in. "Immediately after Dunkirk in 1940," he said, "the British Isles were in effect defenseless so far as organized and equipped ground forces were concerned. Practically all their field army equipment had been lost and an immediate invasion was threatened. . . . For the United States the military issue immediately at stake was the security of the British fleet to dominate the Atlantic."

Churchill appealed to the United States for assistance. He had the manpower, the British soldiers rescued at Dunkirk, but he needed weapons for them.

The United States, in the summer of 1940, was desperately short of weapons itself. It did have, lying about from the First World War, 500,000 Enfield rifles plus some other equipment. This equipment was not modern, but would be needed if the United States suddenly were at war. Could this be given to England? Members of the American general staff argued that providing England with any equipment would be only wasting it. England, they believed, could not last against Germany. That was the expert advice given to Roosevelt.

But FDR was skeptical of it. Knowing something of the sea and something of naval requirements, FDR realized that an invasion of England would require a much greater quantity of small sea craft than Germany had available or had the prospect of acquiring quickly. Also FDR was willing to give more weight to an unmeasurable quality called national spirit than were his military chieftains. He had seen that spirit organize behind him to fight the Depression eight years earlier. He believed he was seeing it mass behind Churchill to fight Germany.

So he rejected the professional military opinion that England would not survive.

"A Supreme Act of Faith"

A 1926 law, which appeared to allow the United States to sell surplus military equipment for cash, was found. With misgivings, George Marshall declared the rifles and the

Before America officially entered World War II, Roosevelt faithfully gave arms support to Britain despite official recommendations not to.

other equipment surplus. Roosevelt was delighted. He told [Secretary of Treasury] Henry Morgenthau to give the shipment of the "surplus" goods priority. "Give it an extra push every morning and every night," he directed, "until it is on board ship!"

"It was," said Churchill of the Roosevelt action, "a supreme act of faith and leadership for the United States to deprive themselves of this very considerable mass of arms for the sake of a country which many deemed already beaten."

After the rifles, the immediate need of England was for destroyers. Churchill asked for the ships in May, 1940. Roosevelt responded that the sale of destroyers required Congressional authorization which, for political reasons, would not be forthcoming. Churchill kept pressing for the ships. After the fall of France, he said, the Germans had the entire French coastline to use as launching sites for submarines, as well as Norway. At the same time German air attacks against British shipping had been serious. In the last ten days of July four British destroyers were sunk and seven were damaged.

"Mr. President," said Winston Churchill, "with great respect I must tell you that in the long history of the world this is a thing to do *now*."

Legal Complications

Franklin Roosevelt resolved to act, but he could not act illegally. Ben Cohen, one of his close aides from the New Deal days and still a government official, told FDR that the destroyers could be released to the British "if their release for such purpose would, as at least some naval authorities believe, strengthen rather than weaken the defense position of the United States."

FDR told Frank Knox that giving the ships, or "releasing" them in Ben Cohen's phrase, would not stand up legally. "Also," he said, "I fear Congress is in no mood at the present time to allow any form of sale." A little later perhaps, FDR suggested to Navy Secretary Knox, Congress might be persuaded to allow the sale of the ships to Canada. This would release Canadian ships to assist England.

But England could not wait. Three weeks after Cohen's memorandum to the President, Churchill informed a sympathetic Henry Morgenthau that "The need of American destroyers is more urgent than ever in view of the losses and the need of coping with the invasion threat.... There is nothing that America can do at this moment that would be of greater help than to send fifty destroyers, except sending one hundred."

A solution was quick to come. A group of the nation's most prestigious lawyers sent a letter to the editor of the *New York Times* in which they claimed that the President had the legal authority to sell over-age destroyers that were then not in use. The letter was developed by Ben Cohen and Dean Acheson. Acheson represented the epitome of the "Washington lawyer." He moved with ease from private practice in the most respected law firms to government service and then back. In the summer of 1940 he was in private practice. He drafted the letter, with Cohen's assistance, and rounded up the signatures. He had no trouble persuading the *New York Times* to publish the letter. Charles Merz, an editor of the newspaper, had been a Yale classmate.

British Reluctance

Robert Jackson, the attorney general, had to be reached and persuaded that the sale could take place without Congressional authorization, then the President had to be persuaded. Neither man required much effort. But curiously, as Jackson later told the story, Winston Churchill did. Rather than sell the ships for money, they would be "sold" for British bases in the Atlantic. The deal was actually a wise one for England. Not only did she receive the ships without having to pay any cash, she was relieved of posting ships at a series of bases in the Atlantic. Also, the placing of American ships at these bases extended America's line of defense into the Atlantic, bringing that line closer to Europe. Still, for a time Churchill feared that the British people would object to the trade, believing that the United States might have taken advantage of their predicament. He continued to press for the giving of the ships to England without any cost.

In a transatlantic telephone conversation with Churchill, Jackson tried to explain that the President had legal authority to sell the ships but did not have the authority to give them.

"Empires just don't bargain," Churchill replied.

"Well," answered the American attorney general, "republics do!"

The President later told Churchill that "The trouble is that I have an attorney general—and he says I have got to make a bargain."

"Maybe," grumbled the Prime Minister in answer, "you ought to trade those destroyers for a new attorney general!"

But the trade went through. America supplied the destroyers and Great Britain leased some of her empire. The President dictated a memorandum on the agreement to send to Congress. When he had finished, he said to his secretary, Grace Tully, as she remembered it: "Grace, Congress is going to raise hell about this but even another day's delay may mean the end of civilization. Cries of 'warmonger' and 'dictator' will fill the air but if Britain is to survive we must act."

Churchill believed the destroyer deal persuaded Spain to remain neutral rather than enter the war on the side of the Axis. He also believed that the deal contributed to Germany and Italy joining with Japan in September, 1940, to organize the Tripartite Pact, as a means of surrounding the United States. Certainly it also made the British understand they were not alone in standing against Adolf Hitler. America was their friend.

Opposition

There was some resistance to assisting England with the rifles and the destroyers. The extreme isolationists and pacifist groups were bitterly opposed. Frederick J. Libby, executive secretary of the National Council for Prevention of War and one of the grand seigniors of the peace movement, charged that the European war would end in a few months unless "direct American participation" prolonged it. "On the continent," Libby said, "Hitler's army, best equipped in history, cannot be defeated."

But Libby and the tiny movement he led were exceptions. Many Americans were willing to aid England, assuming that England paid for such assistance. Part of this was the traditional tie with the Anglo-Saxon nation. Part of it was the abhorrence of the Nazi system. And in 1940 much of it was the shock of the Nazi brutality toward England. Rather than risk invasion, Hitler decided to bomb England into submission. Cities like London and other residential centers were attacked night after night, with civilian and military targets being bombed indiscriminately, in an effort to force England to surrender. But bombing did not produce surrender; rather, it increased the determination to resist.

Sympathy for the victims of this blitz quickly built up in the United States. That sympathy soon would be translated into political action. The politically astute William Allen White [organizer of the Committee to Defend America by Aiding the Allies] wrote to a Congressman friend:

> I have been going to write you for two or three weeks [to tell you] to watch your step about this war from now on. It is approaching England, and anything you say and any vote you cast may possibly have to be defended when the horror of the terrible war is descending upon Great Britain. Public sympathy will be rising for Great Britain and we will forget our isolationist tradition. Watch your step. Your political path is strewn with dy-

namite and step easy and look where you go. The ordinary inhibitions of the last two or three years about your vote on questions of foreign relations are all out. When they begin to bomb Wales and the casualty list of women and children and old men goes into thousands, watch for any vote that would seem to withhold sympathy or aid in that awful time.

This growing sympathy for England made the sale of large supplies of American arms and ammunition that much easier politically. And such sales were substantial. In a report dated February 19, 1941, for example, as the United States faced a request from the British for 900 million rounds of ammunition, George Marshall conceded that "We have to reduce the amount of ammunition for training to about sixty percent" of America's needs. The rationale behind this was the need to keep England fighting. It continued America's first line of defense.

American Industry Prepares for War

There was, however, another side to the large sales of American arms and ammunition to England and to France before it fell to the Germans in 1940. The orders placed by those nations with American firms gave the industries an economic incentive to gear up for military purposes long before Franklin Roosevelt could persuade them to. The Congress might have been reluctant to give FDR needed funds to order arms for American troops, but there was little objection to American industry making a dollar. By the time the American government was ready to move, a firm industrial base for an armaments industry had been created by the British and French orders.

In a little more than two years after entering the war, England spent three billion dollars in the United States for arms. That included two hundred million dollars in direct assistance for capital improvements—buildings, modern machinery—to American corporations. The money went to the makers of airplanes, ammunition, machine tools, motor vehicles, and ships. The American military aircraft industry actually began to develop because of the $1.5 billion in British orders for airplanes placed after September, 1939. What would become famous as the American "Liberty" ship, a quickly-built cargo ship, was begun from a British design and a British contract. The manufacture of American tanks began with United States firms taking contracts to build British tanks. British funds also supplied incentive for the development of a modern machine tool industry and also for the training of skilled workers capable of handling those tools. The American rearmament effort may have been mothered by America's own defensive needs, but it was fathered by the British.

Roosevelt's Attempt to Instigate a War with Germany

Charles Callan Tansill

Because the American people overwhelmingly opposed entering World War II as a combatant, President Roosevelt adopted a strategy that was designed to provoke an incident with the German Navy and force America into the war. In addition to providing material assistance to the Allies, President Roosevelt authorized American ships to escort British ships loaded with war matériel across the Atlantic. In the following essay, historical scholar Charles Callan Tansill writes that by assigning American warships convoy duty, Roosevelt deliberately exposed them to attack from German submarines. Hitler, however, wished desperately to avoid war with the United States and instructed his admirals to avoid engagements with American ships. Even when American naval forces began to act in a decidedly unneutral manner by firing on German ships, Hitler still insisted that his admirals avoid confrontations with the American Navy.

THE NEW AMERICAN NEUTRALITY LAW (NOVEMBER 4, 1939) gave certain satisfaction to Hitler who assured leading Nazis that it would render the United States harmless. Under this law the waters around the British Isles and the entire European coast from Bergen to the Spanish border were closed to American ships. These restrictions pleased the Führer who decreed on December 30, 1939,

---

that American crews were to be treated "with the greatest consideration." In this same spirit Admiral [Erich] Raeder [commander of the German Navy] issued instructions that American ships were not to be pursued or sunk in order that "all difficulties which might result from trade war between the United States and Germany might be avoided at the very beginning." But this German policy of conciliation was sorely tried by incidents arising out of the establishment of a neutrality zone announced by the Panama Conference, October 3, 1939. This safety belt around the Americas south of Canada varied in width from 300 to 1000 miles. Belligerents were warned to refrain from naval action within that area, but no armed forces were stationed along the safety belt to enforce this regulation.

German Conciliation Is Tested

In order to conciliate America the German Admiralty issued orders designed to prevent naval engagements within this safety belt. When the Admiralty wished to recede from this position, Hitler refused to permit any change of orders. Moreover, the Führer adhered to this conciliatory policy even when American vessels adopted a course that must have enraged him. In December 1939 the German liner *Columbus* left Veracruz and was closely trailed by the U.S.S. *Tuscaloosa* which constantly broadcasted her position. This action compelled the Nazi captain to scuttle his ship some 450 miles east of Cape May. The same tactics were pursued by the U.S.S. *Broome* in trailing the *Rhein,* which also was scuttled by her captain. The freighter *Idarwild* was followed by the *Broome* until it was destroyed by H.M.S. *Diomede* (November 1940), with the *Broome* standing by to watch the result of her pursuit. The German Government refrained from filing any protest at these actions.

At a naval conference on March 18, Admiral Raeder was finally able to secure an important concession from the Führer. This took the form of a new blockade order

(March 25, 1941) which not only included Iceland but went as far as the waters of Greenland. The first naval incident in the North Atlantic would soon take place.

The background for such an incident had been carefully filled in by President Roosevelt. In August 1940 he had sent Admiral Robert L. Ghormley, Major General D.C. Emmons, and Major General George V. Strong to London for exploratory conversations concerning eventual "armed cooperation with the British Commonwealth." After some months of conversations with important officers in the British armed services, Admiral Ghormley, in October 1940, sent to Admiral Stark a full report on his mission. Stark, in turn, presented to [Navy] Secretary Knox on November 12 a memorandum on national objectives. One of the most important items in this memorandum was "the prevention of the disruption of the British Empire." In order to achieve this objective, in January 1941 a series of secret staff conversations began in Washington. Two months later (March 27, 1941), the ABC-I Staff Agreement was consummated which envisaged a "full-fledged war co-operation when and if Axis aggression forced the United States into the war."

American Convoys

One of the sections of this agreement was aimed at creating an incident that would "force the United States into the war." It contained the following explosive phraseology: "Owing to the threat to the sea communications of the United Kingdom, the principal task of the United States naval forces in the Atlantic will be the protection of shipping of the Associated Powers." In order to carry out this task the Royal Navy hastened to give the United States Navy the "benefit of its experience, and of the new devices and methods for fighting submarines that had already been evolved." The responsibility "now assumed by the United States Navy meant the organization of a force for escort-of-convoy." On February 1, 1941, this patrol force was given "the new and

Roosevelt Knew Intervention Was Necessary

In the following excerpt John T. Flynn, a journalist during Franklin Roosevelt's presidency, argues that President Roosevelt knowingly led America down the path to involvement in World War II.

The question arose during the [lend-lease] debate: How will we get the arms to Britain? Critics of the President said the next step would have to be convoys to see the arms delivered safely. The President denounced this and said he was opposed to convoys. "Convoys," he had declared, "mean shooting and shooting means war." Yet at that very moment, almost while these words were on his lips, he began convoying.

The truth is that the President had made up his mind to go into the war as early as October, 1940. To believe differently is to write him, our naval chiefs of staff and all our high military and naval officers down as fools. In the

appropriate designation of Atlantic Fleet," and its commander, Rear Admiral Ernest J. King, was promoted to the rank of Admiral and designated Commander in Chief Atlantic Fleet. The first naval incident was almost at hand.

On April 10, 1941, the destroyer *Niblack* (Lieutenant Commander E.R. Durgin), in the waters off Iceland, picked up three boatloads of survivors from a torpedoed Netherlands freighter. As the last men were being pulled aboard, the sound operator made contact on a submarine. The division commander, D.L. Ryan, immediately assumed that the submarine was approaching for an attack so he ordered Mr. Durgin to drop some depth charges which caused the submarine to retire. This was the first action between United States and German armed forces.

First World War it took a gigantic effort to defeat Germany. Then Britain had a million men in France. France had three million in arms. Italy and Russia were our allies. So was Japan. Italy had a million men against Germany, and Russia had four million. Yet with all this Germany was never driven out of France. She surrendered while in possession of most of what she had conquered. Does anyone believe that Roosevelt or [Chief of Staff] General [George] Marshall or any other high military leader thought that England fighting alone could drive Hitler's armies out of France? England did not have a soldier in France. France was prostrate. Her arms factories were in Hitler's possession. Italy was against us rather than for us. So was Japan. The President knew that to drive Hitler out of France it would be necessary to send American armies to France and to send the American navy full blast into the war. And he knew this in October, 1940.

John T. Flynn, *The Roosevelt Myth*. New York: Devon-Adair, 1956.

As the system of convoy escorts developed in accordance with Anglo-American plans, other incidents were bound to occur. On April 17, John O'Donnell, well-known newspaper commentator, published a statement that "battlecraft" of the American Navy and Coast Guard were "giving armed escort to munition-laden British merchantmen leaving American ports." The President, through his secretary, Mr. Early, replied that American naval forces were merely on "neutrality patrol" in the Atlantic. He then charged that Mr. O'Donnell was guilty of a "deliberate lie." On April 25, during a press conference, the President expressly denied that naval escorts were being provided for fleets carrying lend-lease goods, and he developed at great length the difference between patrolling and convoying. A month later (May 27), in a national broadcast, he insisted that the delivery of war matériel to Britain was "imperative" and then stated that he had extended "our patrol in north and south Atlantic waters.". . .

Hitler's Reaction

In the meantime the Führer was showing a strong determination to adhere to his policy of keeping out of war with the United States. In May 1941 the German attitude was summed up at a meeting between Hitler and his naval advisers:

> Whereas up to now the situation confronting submarines and naval forces on operations was perfectly clear, naval warfare in the North Atlantic is becoming increasingly complicated as the result of the measures taken by the U.S.A. In order to help Britain, the American neutrality patrol, which was hitherto confined to the area within the American neutrality zone, has been reinforced and considerably extended toward the east to about 38° W., i.e. as far as the middle of the Atlantic. The true character of the American neutrality patrol is shown by the fact that vessels on patrol have also been instructed to report by radio any battleships encountered. . . .
>
> We have laid down the following rules for naval warfare in order to comply with German political aims with regard to the U.S.A.:
>
> No attack should be made on U.S. naval forces and merchant vessels.
>
> Prize regulations are not to be applied to U.S. merchant ships.
>
> Weapons are not to be used, even if American vessels conduct themselves in a definitely unneutral manner.
>
> Weapons are to be used *only if U.S. ships fire the first shot.*
>
> As a result of these instructions and of the constant endeavors on the part of Germany not to react to provo-

cation, incidents with the U.S.A. have been avoided up to the present time.

It is unmistakable that the U.S. Government is disappointed about this cautious attitude on the part of Germany, since one of the most important factors in preparing the American people for entry into the war is thus eliminated. The U.S. is therefore continuing its attempt to obliterate more and more the boundary line between neutrality and belligerency, and to stretch the "short of war" policy further by constantly introducing fresh measures contrary to international law.

The next naval incident involving German-American relations was the sinking of the American merchant ship (May 21, 1941) *Robin Moor,* New York to Cape Town, by a German submarine. There was no visit or search but the crew and passengers were allowed to take to open lifeboats. As the sinking occurred outside the blockade zone it is evident that the submarine commander disregarded orders concerning American ships. Admiral Raeder immediately issued orders to prevent further incidents of this nature, and Hitler, after confirming these instructions, remarked that he wished to "avoid any incident with the U.S.A." On June 20 the President sent a message to Congress in which he bitterly criticized Germany as an international outlaw. He followed this message with another move in the direction of war. On July 7 he ordered American occupation of Iceland. Two days later Secretary Knox gave a statement to the press which implied that the American patrol force in the North Atlantic had the right to use its guns when the occasion arose.

The *Greer* Incident

This occasion arose on September 4, 1941, when the destroyer *Greer,* bound for Iceland, was informed by a British plane that a submerged U-boat lay athwart her course some ten miles ahead. The *Greer* at once laid a course for the reported submarine, and after having made sound contact with it, kept it on her bow for more than three hours. During this period a British plane dropped four depth charges in the vicinity of the submarine without effect. Finally, the submarine commander grew tired of this game of hide-and-seek and launched a torpedo which the *Greer* was able to dodge. When the *Greer* counterattacked with depth charges, the submarine launched another torpedo which was avoided. When sound contact with the submarine could not be reestablished, the *Greer* resumed course for Iceland.

On September 11 the President gave a broadcast which presented a distorted version of the *Greer* incident. He conveniently forgot to tell that the initiative had been taken by the *Greer*: "She [the *Greer*] was flying the American flag. Her identity as an American ship was unmistakable. She was then and there attacked by a submarine. Germany admits that it was a German submarine. . . . We have sought no shooting war with Hitler. . . . The aggression is not ours. Ours is solely defense." American vessels would now shoot at sight.

In the face of this serious incident that clearly showed the aggressive character of American naval patrolling, Hitler maintained his policy of avoiding difficulties with the United States. On September 17 orders concerning American merchant vessels exempted them from attack, even when in convoy, in all zones except that immediately surrounding the British Isles. In the Pan-American safety belt "no warlike acts" were to be carried out on German initiative.

Escort Duty for American Destroyers

The American answer to these pacific gestures was to authorize escort duty for American destroyers. It was arranged that an American escort group, based on Argentia [Newfoundland, Canada], should take over from a Royal Canadian Navy escort at a designated place off Newfoundland and hand over the convoy to a Royal Navy escort at an agreed mid-ocean meeting place. Convoying was now an established practice, and it should be kept in mind that Secretary Knox, during the lend-lease hearings, had frankly admitted that he regarded convoying as an "act of war."

This *de facto* war in the Atlantic soon produced another incident. On October 16 five American destroyers rushed from Reykjavik, Iceland, to the help of a convoy that was being attacked by submarines. On the following day, while in the midst of the fighting, the destroyer *Kearny* was struck by a torpedo and slowly made its way back to Iceland. It had deliberately moved into the center of a pitched battle between German submarines and British and Canadian warships and had taken the consequences. It was not long before President Roosevelt gave to the American people a twisted account of the incident. On October 27 he recounted the happenings on October 16 and 17 and asserted that he had "wished to avoid shooting." America had "been attacked. The U.S.S *Kearny* is not just a Navy ship. She belongs to every man, woman, and child in this Nation. . . . Hitler's torpedo was directed at every American." In order to give additional overtones of villainy to his description of Nazi wickedness he then stated that he had a secret map made in Germany which disclosed Hitler's plan to put all the continent of South America under his domination. But that was not all. He had in his possession another document made in Germany that revealed Hitler's intention, if he was victorious, to "abolish all existing religions." It should be evident that the "forward march of Hitlerism" should be stopped. . . ."We are pledged to pull our own oar in the destruction of Hitlerism." The American Navy had been given orders to "shoot on sight." The Nazi "rattlesnakes of the sea" would have to be destroyed.

The *Reuben James* Incident

This declaration of war was confirmed by the *Reuben James* incident. On October 31, while the *Reuben James* was escorting a convoy to Iceland, some German submarines were encountered about 600 miles west of that island. The American destroyer was struck by a torpedo and rapidly sank. Only 45, out of a crew of about 160, were saved. When the news of the sinking of the *Reuben James* reached Germany, Hitler remarked: "President Roosevelt has ordered his ships to shoot the moment they sight German ships. I have ordered German ships not to shoot when they sight American vessels but to defend themselves when attacked." On November 13, 1941, the directives for conduct of German warships when encountering American naval vessels remained pacific: "Engagements with American naval or air forces are not to be sought deliberately; they are to be avoided as far as possible. . . . If it is observed before a convoy is attacked that it is being escorted by American forces, the attack is not to be carried out."

Germany was trying desperately to stay out of war with the United States. America's attitude was clearly stated by Sumner Welles at Arlington on November 11: "Beyond the Atlantic a sinister and pitiless conqueror has reduced more than half of Europe to abject serfdom. It is his boast that his system shall prevail even unto the ends of the earth. . . . The American people after full debate . . . have determined upon their policy. They are pledged . . . to spare no effort and no sacrifice in bringing to pass the final defeat of Hitlerism and all that which that evil term implies. . . . We cannot know, we cannot yet foresee, how long and how hard the road may be which leads to that new day when another armistice will be signed."

America at War

To the mind of Welles and to others in the White House group it was obvious that America was really in the war. But the American people did not realize that momentous fact, nor did they know that they were pledged "to spare no effort and no sacrifice in bringing to pass the final defeat of Hitlerism." It was easy for Mr. Welles to speak glibly of sacrifice. He had long enjoyed wealth and high social position. The word "sacrifice" had always been excluded from his dictionary. As the spokesman for the President he was suddenly breaking to the American people the dread news that they had become involved in a war they had ardently wished to avoid.

Roosevelt Provoked the Japanese into War

Patrick J. Buchanan

In the following essay, political commentator and nationally syndicated columnist Patrick J. Buchanan argues that in 1941, Franklin Roosevelt forced the Japanese Empire into a corner from which it had no choice but to yield to American demands or attack. When the Japanese occupied Indochina in 1940, Roosevelt froze all Japanese assets in the United States and cut off Japan's supply of oil. Japanese industry, as well as the Japanese military (then involved in a war with China), was dependent on American oil. The Japanese government indicated a willingness to compromise and offered to meet with Roosevelt to negotiate a peaceful solution, but the Japanese offers were refused. Japan, faced with a choice of backing down in humiliation to American demands or fighting, chose to attack the American fleet at Pearl Harbor.

B Y LATE 1938 THE SINO-JAPANESE WAR HAD REACHED stalemate. Japan's army held the coastal cities, but Chinese nationalists and communists held the interior. When France fell in June 1940, Japan decided to seize its Asian colonies. In September, Tokyo signed the Tripartite Agreement with Germany and Italy, and its army occupied the northern half of French Indochina (Vietnam). Hitler, Stalin, Mussolini, and [Japanese emperor] Hirohito were now all aligned. FDR's response was an embargo on the sale of scrap iron and steel to Japan.

After Hitler invaded the USSR in late June 1940, Japan occupied the rest of Indochina. FDR froze all Japanese assets, thus cutting off trade, including oil. He pressed the British and Dutch to follow. Since Japan's industry and empire were almost totally dependent on oil from the United States and Dutch East Indies, America had just grabbed Japan by the throat. Without oil, Japan could not long continue the war against China; without oil, the Japanese empire must wither and die.

The Danger of Economic Sanctions

Six days before he cut the oil lifeline, FDR was warned in a memo from the navy chief of war plans, Rear Admiral Richmond K. Turner, of the probable consequences:

> It is generally believed that shutting off the American supply of petroleum will lead promptly to an invasion of the Netherlands East Indies [by the Japanese]. . . . Furthermore, it seems certain that, if Japan should then take military measures against the British and Dutch, she would also include military action against the Philippines, which would immediately involve us in a Pacific War.

Given the risks, the recommendation of Turner's report was "that trade with Japan not be embargoed at this time." America's senior naval officer, Admiral Harold Stark, wrote on the report, "I concur in general." Roosevelt himself was fully aware of what an oil embargo meant. Pressed by his interventionists—[Harold] Ickes of Interior, [Henry] Morgenthau of Treasury, and [Henry] Stimson of War—the president gave his cabinet "quite a lecture" on July 18, warning that if the United States "stopped all oil, it would simply drive the Japanese down to the Dutch East Indies, and it would mean war in the Pacific." Yet FDR went ahead. Why? Some historians contend that it was Assistant Secretary of State Dean Acheson who ordered no release of Japanese funds, no more export licenses, thus no sale of oil; and that FDR did not realize the draconian nature of the U.S. sanctions until September. Yet, as Walter Lippmann wrote, "This was a declaration of economic war" on Japan. Tokyo now faced a mortal crisis.

Given Japan's aggression in China, its cruelties, the appalling Rape of Nanking, Tokyo's alliance with Berlin, and its contempt for the Open Door [a policy by which Western imperial powers gained access to Asian trade and resources], America had no obligation to continue providing Japan with the oil that was fueling its navy and army as they rampaged through Asia. But the oil embargo was "economic war" against an oil-starved nation, and FDR had a moral duty to inform the nation he had forced Japan into a corner where Tokyo must yield to America's demands—or attack. This Roosevelt did not do. Why not?

Historians give several explanations. One is that FDR did not realize he had just issued a death sentence on the Japanese empire and it must fight or die. Another is that FDR knew the consequences of an oil embargo and approved, because he wanted Japan to attack. A war with Japan, a member of the Tripartite Pact, was the only way he could take us to war in Europe.

Maneuvering America into the War

When, exactly, FDR decided to shift U.S. policy from all-out aid short of war to taking America into war is difficult to place. But once reelected in November 1940, his rhetoric and actions became openly belligerent. FDR seemed to court a conflict. But while he seemed anxious, even desperate, to get into the war, the nation he had been elected to lead, on a promise to stay out, wanted to stay out. Surveyed in August 1941 on the question, "If you were asked to vote today on the question of the United States going to war against Japan, how would you vote?" Americans, by 76 percent to 24 percent, said, "Stay out." As late as October 22, seven weeks before Pearl Harbor, Americans by 74 percent to 13 percent were against going to war with Japan. The American people in the fall of 1941 did not believe that who controlled China or French Indochina was worth fighting about.

On November 25, 1941, Secretary of War Henry L. Stimson confided to his diary that the question of the hour was "how we should maneuver them into the position of firing the first shot." Stimson and FDR knew their history. Only after the Mexican army had killed U.S. soldiers north of the Rio Grande did [President James K.] Polk ask for a declaration of war. Only after the South had fired on Fort Sumter did Lincoln put out a call for volunteers. Only after Germany had sunk four U.S. merchant ships in 1917 did Wilson deliver his war message. FDR needed to maneuver Japan into firing the first shot.

Last Chance for Peace

Through the summer and into the fall of 1941, Japan sought a way out. Tokyo offered to withdraw from southern Indochina and not to join Germany in an offensive war if the United States would lift the embargo and tell China to negotiate. The United States rejected the offer. Prince Fumimaro Konoye, Japan's prime minister and leader of the peace party, offered to meet FDR anywhere in the Pacific. In a three-hour secret meeting with Ambassador Joseph Grew, Konoye confided that ranking officers in the army and navy were behind him and would accompany him to Juneau, Alaska, and his ship would be equipped with special telephone lines to the emperor, who, said Grew, "would immediately issue a rescript ordering the suspension forthwith of all hostile operations" in China and Indochina. Ambassador Grew wrote in his memoirs:

> We in the Embassy had no doubt that the Prime Minister would have agreed, at his meeting with the President, to the eventual withdrawal of all Japanese forces from all of Indochina and from all of China with the face-saving expedient of being permitted to retain a

limited number of troops in North China and Inner Mongolia temporarily.

Grew believed the United States was on the verge of a diplomatic triumph, without war. But Secretary of State Cordell Hull, fearing a "second Munich," rebuffed the offer. Though the president initially showed interest, he deferred to Hull, and began setting preconditions for any meeting. Konoye was soon replaced by [Hideki] Tojo, and the opportunity was gone. . . .

The Day of Reckoning

On November 26, 1941, Washington told Tokyo America's nonnegotiable demands for lifting the embargo stood: total withdrawal from Indochina and China, acceptance of Chinese sovereignty, and cancellation of Tokyo's tripartite pact with Germany and Italy. Japan's dependence on trade for the necessities of national life had left the empire at the mercy of the United States.

Thus came the day of reckoning for the Empire of the Sun. Tokyo's options were now reduced to two: diplomatic surrender and humiliating retreat from Indochina and China, meaning an end to Japan's day as a Great Power— or a desperate lunge south to seize the vital resources for which Japan was starving. Tokyo chose the second course. But to succeed, Japan had to neutralize the one force in the Pacific that could block a drive south: the U.S. battle fleet riding at anchor at Pearl Harbor.

Its only chance of victory, Japan believed, was to strike first, as at Port Arthur, cripple U.S. naval power, capture the Philippines, seize the oil and minerals to make Japan self-sufficient, expand the empire to its limit, and then, behind a ring of navy steel, negotiate a truce with the United States. Not until the American rebuff of November 26 did Japan abandon hope in negotiations, but two months before, it had begun to prepare for the possibility that talks

would fail. On September 6, 1941, at an imperial conference, Japan's leaders had ordered preparations for war.
Premier Konoye wrote in his memoirs what had been
agreed upon:

> The Empire shall perfect war preparations generally by
> the latter part of October with a determination to be
> prepared for war with America, England, and The
> Netherlands in order to assure its independent national
> existence and self-defense. . . .
>
> In case there is no expectation of achievement of our
> demands by . . . diplomatic measures within the first ten
> days of October, decision shall be made to go to war.

The army needed an October decision to have troops
and shipping assembled to strike by the end of November.
Japan's hope of victory now rested on an imperial navy
made superior in the western Pacific by U.S. failure to
match Japanese naval construction after Tokyo broke out
of the Washington treaty limits in 1934. In December 1941
Japan had eleven aircraft carriers to six for the United
States, and three of the U.S. carriers were assigned to the
Atlantic. America had ceded to Japan something it could
never have achieved on its own: a fighting chance to defeat
the United States in a naval war. The United States had 29
percent of world manufacturing to Japan's 3.8 percent, but
had failed to translate its industrial might into military
power. Here was the Pacific balance in December of 1941:

	Japan	U.S.	England	Netherlands
Aircraft Carriers	11	3	0	0
Battleships	10	9	2	0
Heavy Cruisers	18	13	1	0
Light Cruisers	23	11	7	3

	Japan	U.S.	England	Netherlands
Destroyers	129	80	13	7
Submarines	67	56	0	13

Reviewing this power equation, weighing the ig-
nominy of retreat against the possibility of glorious victory, Emperor Hirohito authorized his new premier, Hideki
("Razor Brain") Tojo, to launch the attack. On December 8
FDR went before Congress to decry "a date which will live
in infamy." The same day, former President Hoover wrote
to friends, "You and I know that this continuous putting
pins in rattlesnakes finally got this country bitten."

Roosevelt Did Not Provoke the Japanese into War

Nathan Miller

Some historians have charged that Franklin Roosevelt's desire to involve America in World War II drove him to provoke the Japanese to attack the United States, thereby getting America into the war through the "back door." According to journalist and historian Nathan Miller, this assessment of Roosevelt's foreign policy is flawed. Roosevelt's attention was focused on events in Europe and the president felt that a war in the Pacific was the wrong war at the wrong time. A conflict with Japan would drain vital resources from the goal that Roosevelt placed above all others—the defeat of Hitler. Though the Japanese attacked first, Roosevelt focused the American war effort against Nazi Germany. Moreover, nothing in the Tripartite Pact—the treaty signed by Japan, Germany, and Italy—required Germany to come to Japan's aid in case of war.

ISOLATIONISTS, REVISIONIST HISTORIANS, AND ROOSEVELT-haters—sometimes one and the same—have built an industry based upon proving that the Japanese attack on Pearl Harbor was a monstrous conspiracy hatched in the Oval Office. This devil theory holds that Roosevelt provoked the Japanese in order to drag the United States into World War II through the back door when Hitler would not oblige him with a declaration of war. To unite the

Excerpted from *F.D.R.: An Intimate History*, by Nathan Miller (New York: Meridian, 1983). Copyright ©1983 by Nathan Miller. Reprinted by permission of the Estate of Nathan Miller.

American people behind him, conspiracy theorists charge, the master plotter in the White House connived by acts of commission and omission to create an incident in the Pacific. Pearl Harbor rescued Roosevelt from an impossible dilemma, but this is a far cry from proof that he plotted to provoke the Japanese. And even if Roosevelt wished Japan to strike first, it seems hardly likely that he would have offered up the Pacific Fleet as a sacrifice—particularly when he would need these same ships to win the war.

The Wrong War at the Wrong Time

A war in the Pacific was the wrong war at the wrong time in the wrong ocean, as far as Roosevelt was concerned. The basic thrust of his policy was to keep Britain afloat—preferably by all means short of war—and war with Japan would drain off men and matériel from operations against Germany, which was perceived as the main enemy. Roosevelt hoped to deter the Japanese aggression by such moves as transferring the Pacific Fleet to Pearl Harbor from its previous base, at San Pedro, California. In fact, the ABC-I Plan secretly worked out by the military and naval staffs of the United States, Britain, and Canada in March 1941 established a "Europe First" strategy. If the United States became involved in a two-ocean war, Japan was to be held in check through defensive operations until Hitler had been defeated and the Allies were ready to deal with her. American policy in the Far East was to tighten the economic screws on Japan while avoiding a shooting war because of the weakness of the Pacific Fleet, which had fewer ships of every type than the Japanese Navy, following the transfers to the Atlantic. "I simply have not got enough Navy to go around," Roosevelt complained.

The conspiracy theory is also undermined by the lack of any assurance that even if Japan was provoked into an attack against the United States, war with Germany would result. Nothing in the Tripartite Pact, which Japan had signed with Germany and Italy, required the signatories to come to the aid of the others in case of war. Japan used this loophole to escape joining its Axis partner in the attack on the Soviet Union, so why should Hitler assist his less than faithful ally? If he had not declared war on the United States for his own reasons, it would have been a master-stroke. The Americans and British would have been trapped into a war in the Far East that would have divided British strength and diverted American arms and supplies from the European front.

Miscalculations

In the final analysis, the Pacific war resulted from the mis-calculation by Japan and the United States of the inten-tions of each other. Both wanted peace, but they had dif-ferent definitions of what constituted peace. To the Americans, it meant a cessation of Japanese aggression in China and elsewhere; to the Japanese, it meant an East Asia dominated by Japan. These were the hard-core positions from which the nation could not retreat. Surely, said the Japanese, the Americans should understand that a modern industrial nation must have access to raw materials and markets. The control of Manchuria, China, Southeast Asia—the Greater East Asia Co-Prosperity Sphere—was absolutely essential to Japan's existence as a first-rate in-dustrial power. American policy, on the other hand, con-fused morality with reality. As a result of the popular ide-alization of China, the United States allowed the keystone of its policy in the Far East to be based upon an issue that was extraneous to its basic interests: the liberation of China. Never believing that Japan would commit national suicide by going to war with the Western powers, Roosevelt was convinced that through firmness he could force the Japanese to moderate their course. By the end of 1940, the United States had cut off all shipments of all vital war matériel to Japan except for petroleum.

Would concessions by the United States have placated the Japanese? Gordon W. Prange, who has made the most complete study of the events preceding Pearl Harbor, thinks not. Japanese policy had its own dynamic, he pointed out, and American concessions were regarded as weaknesses that invited further demands. Bogged down in China, Japan desperately needed the oil and mineral wealth of Southeast Asia and the Dutch East Indies to keep its military machine running. The summer of 1941 seemed a favorable time for expansion. British forces were being pushed back in North Africa, the Russians were reeling under the German offensive, and American eyes were fixed on the grim events unfolding in the Atlantic.

The Japanese Drive South

The drive to the south began in July 1941, with the occupation of Indochina, including the fine harbor at Camranh Bay, only seven hundred fifty miles from Singapore. The feeble Vichy regime, which ruled a prostrate France, acquiesced without resistance. Warning lights flashed in Washington. The Japanese advance was viewed as a preliminary to an eventual attack on the Philippines, Malaya, and the Dutch East Indies. The Americans knew what was coming, because a code-breaking operation known as Magic was reading the Japanese diplomatic, or Purple, code. Admiral Kichisaburo Nomura, the Japanese ambassador, was summoned to the White House on July 24, where, flanked by [Sumner] Welles, acting Secretary of State in the absence of the ailing [Cordell] Hull, and Admiral Stark, the Chief of Naval Operations, the President issued a stern warning. The Dutch would resist any Japanese attempt to seize the oil of the East Indies, the British would come to their assistance, he declared, "and in view of our own policy of assisting Great Britain, an exceedingly serious situation would immediately result." This bitter pill had a sugar coating. If Japan withdrew from Indochina, the region would be neutralized and the Japanese would be guaranteed free access to its rice and raw materials. Roosevelt had little hope the offer would be accepted but regarded it as "one more effort to avoid Japanese expansion to [the] South Pacific."

Roosevelt Freezes Japanese Assets

Two days later, having heard nothing from Tokyo, the President delivered a body blow to the Japanese economy. He issued an executive order freezing some $131 million in Japanese assets in the United States, which ended trade between the two countries—trade that included 80 percent of Japan's oil consumption. Roosevelt had no desire to strangle Japan, however. Not long afterward, Washington indicated that export licenses would be granted for low-octane petroleum products that were unsuitable for production of aviation gasoline. Fearing that a complete embargo would trigger a Japanese invasion of the East Indies, "the President was still unwilling to draw the noose tight," said [Secretary of the Interior Harold] Ickes. "He thought it might be better to . . . give it a jerk now and then."

The British and the Dutch followed up on the American embargo by refusing to sell oil to Japan—a move that was viewed by the angry Japanese as the last step in the encirclement of the empire by the Western powers.

Like strategists in all eras, the Japanese had prepared for the next war in terms of the last one. In case of a conflict with the United States, they planned to use their fleet to capture the Philippines, strike for the East Indies, and then confront the advancing Americans in a climactic battle in the Japanese-controlled waters of the Central Pacific. But, early in 1941, Admiral Isoroku Yamamoto, Commander in Chief of the Combined Fleet, conceived a much more daring plan. Having observed America's industrial might at first hand as a student at Harvard and then as a naval attaché in Washington, he declared that Japan had no hope of winning a

Roosevelt Rallies the Nation to War

In the following fireside chat of December 9, 1941—two days after the Japanese attack on the American Pacific Fleet at Pearl Harbor—President Roosevelt calls on all Americans to aid in the fight against the Axis menace.

My fellow Americans. The sudden criminal attacks perpetrated by the Japanese in the Pacific provide the climax of a decade of international immorality.

Powerful and resourceful gangsters have banded together to make war upon the whole human race. Their challenge has now been flung at the United States of America. The Japanese have treacherously violated the long-standing peace between us. Many American soldiers and sailors have been killed by enemy action. American ships have been sunk; American airplanes have been destroyed. . . .

I can say with utmost confidence that no Americans, today or a thousand years hence, need feel anything but pride in our patience and in our efforts through all the years toward achieving a peace in the Pacific which

war with the United States unless the U.S. Pacific Fleet, which was in Hawaiian waters, could be destroyed. . . .

Stalling for Time

During the four months between the oil embargo and the Pearl Harbor raid, both sides engaged in a ponderous diplomatic ballet designed to gain time. Roosevelt told Churchill that he hoped "to baby" the Japanese along, for the longer the United States managed to avoid a war with Japan, the better the chances for an incident to occur in the Atlantic. Time was needed to build up defenses in the Pacific, especially in the Philippines, where the armed forces would be fair and honorable to every nation, large or small. And no honest person, today or a thousand years hence, will be able to suppress a sense of indignation and horror at the treachery committed by the military dictators of Japan, under the very shadow of the flag of peace borne by their special envoys in our midst.

The course that Japan has followed for the past ten years in Asia has paralleled the course of Hitler and Mussolini in Europe and in Africa. Today, it has become far more than a parallel. It is collaboration, actual collaboration, so well calculated that all the continents of the world, and all the oceans, are now considered by the Axis strategists as one gigantic battlefield. . . .

We are now in this war. We are all in it—all the way. Every single man, woman, and child is a partner in the most tremendous undertaking of our American history. We must share together the bad news and the good news, the defeats and the victories—the changing fortunes of war.

Franklin D. Roosevelt, Fireside Chat, December 9, 1941.

had recently been federalized, with Douglas MacArthur placed in command. Japan's civilian leadership sought time to find a diplomatic solution that would appease the militarists and avoid war, while the military in turn used the interval to perfect their preparations for war.

Prince Fumimaro Konoye, the Japanese Premier, requested a summit meeting with Roosevelt, preferably in Hawaii. The President, with his fondness for personal diplomacy, leaned toward accepting the proposal, but Secretary Hull, convinced that Konoye would be unable to offer significant concessions, opposed the meeting. Indeed, he argued that by raising false hopes it would be worse than no meeting at all and would have a crushing effect upon China's will to resist. Most analysts now believe that Roosevelt should have met Konoye, for even if they were unable to reach a settlement, the timetable for the Pearl Harbor attack would probably have been set back. By the time it got on track again, it might have been clear to the Japanese that the Soviet Union was not going to collapse and that an attack on the Allies was a dangerous proposition.

Tojo's Reply

The Konoye government did not survive the American rejection of the summit. In mid-October, the Premier told General Hideki Tojo, the War Minister and a leading militant, that unless Japan agreed "in principle" to withdraw its troops from China, there was no possibility of a diplomatic settlement with the United States. Tojo declared that the Army would never agree to an end to the "China Incident" on such terms, and Konoye resigned. The Army would not agree to a civilian as Premier, and the Emperor appointed Tojo, who also remained as Minister of War. To appease the Emperor, who resisted the idea of war, Tojo dispatched a proposal to Washington on November 5, which constituted Japan's final offer. If no accord was reached by November 25, a deadline extended to November 29, hostilities would begin. The actual date for the raid on Pearl Harbor was fixed for December 7 Hawaiian time.

In Washington, the Magic code breakers read the Japanese proposals before they were presented by Admiral Nomura and Saburo Kurusu, a special emissary sent from Tokyo, and they contained nothing new. Japan expressed a willingness to withdraw its troops from Southeast Asia, but first the United States must agree to cease all aid to China and end the oil embargo. The envoys were met by Hull with sermons on the need for law and justice in the Pacific. Roosevelt told Ickes that "he wished he knew whether Japan was playing poker or not. He was not sure whether or not Japan had a gun up its sleeve." To Ickes, it seemed that "the President had not yet reached the state of mind where he is willing to be aggressive as to Japan." The small circle privy to the Magic intercepts became increasingly nervous as Nomura and Kurusu received repeated warnings from Tokyo that they had only until November 29 to reach an accord, because "things are automatically going to happen" afterward. Security surrounding the Pearl Harbor operation was so tight that neither man was aware that the strike force—six carriers and two battleships—had slipped away into the fog of the North Pacific.

Modus Vivendi

Wishing to make one last attempt to stem the inexorable drift toward war, Roosevelt proposed an accommodation, or *modus vivendi*, with the Japanese, intended to return the situation in the Far East to the status quo of July 1941. The oil embargo would be lifted and talks between China and Japan initiated. In return, Japan would send no further troops to Indochina or along the Manchurian frontier with the Soviet Union and agree not to invoke the Tripartite Pact even if the United States went to war with Germany and Italy. "I am not very hopeful and we must all be prepared for real trouble, possibly soon," Roosevelt told [British prime minister Winston] Churchill on November 24. The following day, the President discussed the possibility of a Japanese surprise attack with his War Council: Hull, [Secretary of Navy Frank] Knox, [Secretary of War Henry] Stimson, and his military and naval advisers. "The question was how we should maneuver them into the position of firing the first shot without allowing too much danger to ourselves," observed Stimson. Conspiracy theorists have seized upon the statement as incontrovertible proof that Roosevelt planned to trick the Japanese into attacking the United States, but Stimson later explained that he meant that to have the full support of the American people, it was absolutely necessary to leave no doubt as to who was the aggressor.

Roosevelt's plan for a *modus vivendi* collapsed when the Chinese expressed alarm, fearing that any agreement made with the Japanese would be at their expense. "What about Chiang Kai-shek?" asked Churchill. "Is he not having a very thin diet?" The President might have pressed ahead anyway if he had seen a glimmer of hope, but on the morning of November 26, Stimson barged in, while Roosevelt was still holding bedside court, with the news that a large convoy of Japanese troopships had been sighted steaming south from Formosa. Roosevelt "fairly blew up," Stimson reported. "That changed the whole situation because it was evidence of bad faith on the part of the Japanese," he declared. "While they were negotiating for an entire truce—an entire withdrawal—they should [not] be sending that expedition down there to Indo-China." The truce plan was angrily withdrawn and Hull countered with a ten-point proposal that reiterated principles that Japan had previously rejected. "I have washed my hands of it," Hull said, according to Stimson, "and it is now in the hands of you and Knox—the Army and Navy." . . .

Throughout the first week of December, there was a feeling in Washington that some implacable machine had been placed in gear and no one knew how to stop it. Hull continued his unfruitful conversations with Nomura and Kurusu as they awaited a reply to the Ten-Point Plan. Congressional leaders were requested not to suspend sessions for more than three days at a time. The President met daily with the War Council. Intelligence reports of Japanese ship movements filtered in, and Magic revealed that the Foreign Office in Tokyo had advised its embassies to burn their diplomatic codes, a sure sign of an impending rupture of relations. But there was no sign of the Pearl Harbor attack force because the ships maintained strict radio silence during the entire voyage. . . .

Roosevelt Appeals to the Emperor

Roosevelt made a personal appeal for peace to Emperor Hirohito on December 6. Kurusu had told him this was the only way to prevent war. "Both of us for the sake of the peoples not only of our own great countries but for the sake of humanity in neighboring territories, have a sacred duty to restore traditional amity and prevent further death and destruction to the world," he wrote.

"This son of man has just sent his final message to the Son of God," he told some dinner guests after the message was on its way. Lord Halifax, the British ambassador, was assured that in case of an attack on British or Dutch territory "we should obviously all be together." Later that evening, the President and Hopkins were in the Oval Study when a special courier brought Magic intercepts of the first thirteen parts of a fourteen-part Japanese reply to the American proposal. The message instructed the emissaries to inform the United States Government that the proposal had been rejected. Roosevelt read it through in about ten minutes while Hopkins nervously paced the floor.

"This means war," the President declared as he passed the message along to Hopkins.

"Since war was undoubtly going to come at the convenience of the Japanese," Hopkins replied, "it was too bad that we could not strike the first blow and prevent any sort of surprise."

"No, we can't do that," said the President. "We are a democracy and peaceful people."

A few hours later, halfway around the globe in the Central Pacific, six aircraft carriers flying the sunburst flag of Japan turned into the wind to launch their deadly brood. As the first plane roared down the flight deck of the flagship *Akagi* into the dawning sky, the crew sped it on its way with three ceremonial *Banzais*. Within fifteen minutes, 183 bombers, fighters, and torpedo planes were headed south toward Pearl Harbor, about two hundred thirty miles away.

CHAPTER
4

ROOSEVELT'S TREATMENT OF MINORITIES

Roosevelt's Reluctant Support of African Americans

Harvard Sitkoff

In the following essay, University of New Hampshire history professor Harvard Sitkoff describes the limited but nevertheless groundbreaking advancements made on behalf of African Americans during Franklin D. Roosevelt's presidency. Although segregation and discrimination remained a fact of life in America, the Roosevelt administration aided blacks to an unprecedented extent. New Deal proponents joined civil rights advocates in a largely successful struggle for equal treatment in Roosevelt's recovery programs. The number of African American federal employees tripled during Roosevelt's presidency and over one hundred African Americans were appointed to administrative posts by FDR. Though many of Roosevelt's attempts to provide equality for African Americans were halfhearted, his efforts stimulated hope for the civil rights movement and raised the expectations of African Americans.

F OR THREE CENTURIES RACISM HAD INFECTED THE NATION-al mind as well as the body politic. No labor leader, no public official, could ignore the results. The majority of white Americans wanted no change in race relations. They favored neither desegregation nor equal opportunities for blacks. Millions remained enslaved by fear, ignorance, and prejudice, and their emancipation continued to be a

Excerpted from *A New Deal for Blacks: The Emergence of Civil Rights as a National Issue*, vol. 1, *The Depression Decade*, by Harvard Sitkoff. Copyright ©1981 by Oxford University Press, Inc. Used by permission of Oxford University Press, Inc.

dream deferred, as it did for most blacks. The majority of Afro-Americans stayed trapped in what Oscar Lewis would later call the "culture of poverty." Plagued by illiteracy, social disorganization, physical isolation, disfranchisement, and their "mark of oppression," most Negroes could not yet battle for full citizenship or rebel against the inequities destroying them.

It would take a quarter of a century of prosperity, a world war and a protracted cold war, the end of white colonialism in Africa, and a mass exodus of blacks from the South that would dwarf all such migration prior to 1940 before the basic conditions of life for blacks would change significantly. Those same developments would also make it possible for individuals, organizations, and movements to alter relations between the races to an extent not conceivable in the thirties. Even in the 1970s, moreover, racial equality would not be achieved. The goal of ending discrimination and racial injustice remained unfulfilled. To ignore this and to condemn those who assisted the black freedom struggle for failing to end racism in the 1930s is a judgment beyond history. Such an evaluation recapitulates the error of many liberals in the thirties who did not comprehend the persistence and depth of white supremacy. They believed it could be easily overcome. We should know better.

"A New Type of Faith"

But something vital did begin in the thirties. Negro expectations rose; black powerlessness decreased; white hostility diminished. Together, these gave the proponents of civil rights hope, what the Philadelphia *Tribune* termed "the emergence of a new type of faith."

Alongside the continuity of discrimination and segregation, the federal government aided blacks to an unprecedented extent, both substantively and symbolically. New Dealers joined with civil rights organizations to fight for equality of treatment for blacks in the relief and recovery programs and largely succeeded in the Farm Security Administration (FSA), National Youth Administration (NYA), Public Works Administration (PWA), United States Housing Authority (USHA), and Federal Works Agency (FWA). The quota system instituted by [Secretary of the Interior Harold] Ickes became a model for the President's Committee on Fair Employment Practices and numerous other federal and state agencies to follow in their efforts to guarantee blacks a fair deal. The number of Afro-American federal employees tripled in the depression decade. Over a hundred Negroes were appointed to administrative posts by Roosevelt. The administration began the desegregation of federal restrooms, cafeterias, and secretarial pools. In addition, a host of government publications and conferences focused on "the Negro problem." They made explicit the federal government's responsibility for and recognition of issues of human rights. Never before, moreover, had a First Lady and so many high level government officials associated so closely with the civil rights movement. However half-heartedly, President Roosevelt also endorsed the campaigns for anti–poll tax and anti-lynching legislation. The most prominent whites in the nation had started to legitimate the aspirations of blacks on a wide variety of issues.

Civil Rights Become a New Deal Matter

President Roosevelt's appointments further stimulated hope for racial changes. The presence of a Black Cabinet and such men as Will Alexander, Harry Hopkins, Harold Ickes, and Aubrey Williams helped to make civil rights a New Deal matter. "The worst fears of the unregenerate South are being realized," [William] Hastie concluded at the end of the decade. "It seems that the U.S. Senate is the last stronghold of the Confederacy." With the exception of James Byrnes, Roosevelt's eight selections for the Supreme Court

Eleanor Roosevelt stands next to Mary McLeod Bethune at the Second National Conference on Negro Youth in January of 1939. Both President and Mrs. Roosevelt were advocates for civil rights and showed their support for the movement in a variety of ways.

became pronounced partisans of civil rights. Indeed, what would culminate in the Warren Court clearly began in the Roosevelt Court. Its decisions in cases involving the exclusion of blacks from juries, the right to picket against discrimination in employment, inequality in interstate transportation, disfranchisement, racial restrictive covenants, and discrimination in the payment of Negro teachers and the admission of blacks to graduate education made the Afro-American less a *freedman* and more a *free man*. Equally important, the Court circumscribed the boundaries of permissible discrimination by its federalizing of the Bill of Rights and its expansion of the concept of state action. It signaled the demise of *Plessy v. Ferguson* [a Supreme Court decision that legitimized Jim Crow practices in the South] by insisting on inquiring into the facts of segregation, rather than just the theory.

The lessening of deference to Southern Democrats by Northern liberals on the race issue also buoyed the expectations of civil rights proponents. The prominence of Dixie Democrats in the conservative coalition and the decline of the power of the South within the Democratic party caused urban liberals to reevaluate their traditional support for their Southern colleagues in opposition to civil rights. The growth of the black vote in the North and the identification of racism with fascism, both at home and abroad, necessitated a switch. So did the endorsement of civil rights legislation by major Popular Front, labor, and liberal organizations. In 1922 only 8 Democrats broke party regularity to vote in favor of the Dyer anti-lynching bill. In 1937, however, when the House again voted on the issue, 171 of the 185 Northern and Western Democrats recorded deserted the South to vote aye.

The hopefulness of black leaders that [Paul] Robeson [a popular black actor and a vocal supporter of African American rights] referred to similarly reflected the changes in the radical left and labor movements. Prior to the thirties, both had been indifferent or opposed to the Afro-Americans' quest for civil rights. By the end of the depression decade they were preaching the egalitarian gospel to millions of white Americans. The Communists and the Congress of Industrial Organizations (CIO), in particular, became the loudest advocates of economic, political, and social equality for blacks, and the best-organized and financed proponents of Negro rights. In countless ways, they emphasized the need for interracial unity and proved it could work.

The politics of self-interest, far more than altruism or

paternalism, had ended the isolation of blacks in their struggle for racial justice. As Malcolm Cowley witnessed: "Negroes no longer stand alone." Alongside them stood radicals pressing for class unity unhampered by racial divisions; labor leaders wanting strong unions; ethnic and political minorities desiring greater security for themselves from a strong central government that would protect constitutional rights; and liberals battling opponents of the New Deal. Civil rights became a stick with which to beat Southern conservatism. . . .

The civil rights movement benefited from these developments. Both black separatism and Negro conservatism lost ground. A new black leadership emerged. Aggressive advocates of racial equality and an end to segregation, such as Walter White, Lester Granger, A. Philip Randolph, and Adam Clayton Powell, Jr., became the chief spokesmen for black America. They sought for blacks all the rights, privileges, and opportunities enjoyed by whites. Working in conjunction with their new white allies, they gained an unprecedented amount of political punch, financial resources, and access to the major institutions shaping public opinion and policy. A mounting number of blacks and whites, consequently, began to listen to the movement and to respond.

Roosevelt's responses to the black demands of 1940 and 1941 indicated the extent of change in the civil rights movement since the beginning of the depression. The views of the National Association for the Advancement of Colored People (NAACP) or of Mary Bethune [an advocate of African American rights and confidant of Eleanor Roosevelt] could no longer be ignored. Roosevelt believed that he had to meet them halfway. His decision to establish the President's Committee on Fair Employment Practices reflected the intensification of Negro militancy as well as the importance of the black vote in national elections. It also mirrored his awareness of the liberalization of attitudes toward the rights of blacks that had occurred in the preceding decade. President Roosevelt's Executive Order 8802 in 1941, the first such proclamation on Negro rights since Reconstruction, measured the distance traveled by the movement. It symbolized a coming of age for civil rights. Yet Roosevelt's actions also pointed to the limits of change. He presented the proponents of racial reform with the weakest possible Fair Employment Practices Committee (FEPC). He understood that however much black powerlessness had been diminished in the thirties, the advocates of racial equality could not yet counter the strength of the forces arrayed against change. White hostility had been dented, but not overcome.

"We Are on Our Way"

Still, the hopes of blacks for a better tomorrow mounted. Many believed along with Bethune that "we are on our way." Virtually every speech and article by the proponents of the black struggle at the end of the New Deal era looked forward with optimism. They saw in urbanization, in increasing education, in involvement in the labor movement and politics, and in support by white allies the social base for a growing civil rights movement. Most commented on the fact that blacks no longer accepted white superiority or their own plight. Some stressed the lessons learned through mass action about establishing networks of influence and information. All emphasized the awakening of Afro-Americans to the possibility of change, the belief that a new page in American history had been turned.

The soil had been tilled. The seeds that would later bear fruit had been planted. They would continue to be nurtured by the legal and political developments, the ideas articulated, the alliances formed, and the expectations raised during the New Deal years. The sprouts of hope prepared the ground for the struggles to follow. Harvest time would come in the next generation.

The Internment of Japanese Americans Was Justified

William H. Rehnquist

In the following essay, Chief Justice of the United States William H. Rehnquist analyzes the three Supreme Court decisions— *Hirabayashi v. United States, Korematsu v. United States,* and *Endo v. United States*—that upheld the constitutionality of the government's removal of Japanese Americans from areas on the west coast. Concurring with the Supreme Court decisions, Rehnquist explains that in the wake of the Japanese attack at Pearl Harbor, the Roosevelt administration's relocation of Japanese Americans was justified. Though hindsight reveals the relocation measures to be harsh and based on racist attitudes, the destruction of the Pacific Fleet at Pearl Harbor left the west coast vulnerable to attack by Japanese bombers flying from aircraft carriers positioned off the coast, if not actual invasion by Japanese ground forces. Moreover, American aircraft production was highly concentrated on the west coast and there was evidence that residents of Japanese ancestry, loyal to Japan, had been placed in the aircraft plants.

T HE JUDGMENT OF POSTWAR PUBLIC OPINION WAS THAT the forced relocation and detention of people of Japanese ancestry was a grave injustice to the great majority who were loyal to the United States. Eugene Rostow, then a professor at Yale Law School and later its dean, writing in

---

Excerpted from *All the Laws but One*, by William H. Rehnquist. Copyright ©1998 by William H. Rehnquist. Reprinted by permission of Alfred A. Knopf, a division of Random House, Inc.

1945, declared the program "a disaster." He criticized it as representing an abandonment of our traditional subordination of military to civil authority, and as sanctioning racially based discrimination against those of Japanese ancestry. Edward Ennis, who as a lawyer in the Justice Department had opposed the adoption of the program, reappeared nearly forty years later on behalf of the American Civil Liberties Union to testify before the congressionally created commission investigating this wartime episode. He characterized the program as "the worst blow to civil liberty in our history."

In the view of the present author, some of this criticism is well justified, and some not; its principal fault is that it lumps together the cases of the Issei—immigrants from Japan—and the Nisei—children of those immigrants who were born in the United States and citizens of the United States by reason of that fact.

The cases [challenging the constitutionality of Japanese relocation] before the Supreme Court—*Hirabayashi* [*v. United States*], *Korematsu* [*v. United States*], and *Endo* [*v. United States*]—all involved Nisei. The basis on which the Court upheld the plan was military representations as to the necessity for evacuation. These representations were undoubtedly exaggerated, and they were based in part on the view that not only the Issei but the Nisei were different from other residents of the west coast.

In defense of the military, it should be pointed out that these officials were not entrusted with the protection of anyone's civil liberties; their task instead was to make sure that vital areas were as secure as possible from espionage or sabotage. The role of General DeWitt, the commander of the west coast military department, was not one to encourage a nice calculation of the costs in civil liberties as opposed to the benefits to national security. Contributing to this attitude would have been the news that General Walter Short, the army commander in Hawaii, and Admi-

Proper Security Measures

Fred Korematsu was a Japanese American who refused to leave his home in San Leandro, California, following a military order excluding "all persons of Japanese ancestry." Korematsu challenged the government's right to evict him from his home and in 1944 his case, Korematsu v. United States, was argued before the Supreme Court. The Court ruled against Korematsu and Supreme Court Justice Hugo Black defended the government's relocation of Japanese Americans against charges of racism.

It is said that we are dealing here with the case of imprisonment of a citizen in a concentration camp solely because of his ancestry, without evidence or inquiry concerning his loyalty and good disposition towards the United States. Our task would be simple, our duty clear, were this a case involving the imprisonment of a loyal citizen in a concentration camp because of racial prejudice. Regardless of the true nature of the assembly and relocation centers—and we deem it unjustifiable to call them concentration camps with all the ugly connotations that term implies—we are dealing specifically with

ral Husband E. Kimmel, the navy commander there, were both summarily removed from their commands ten days after Pearl Harbor because of their failure to anticipate the Japanese surprise attack. DeWitt was surely going to err on the side of caution in making his calculations. . . .

The United States prides itself on a system in which the civilian heads of the service departments are supreme over the military chiefs, so one might expect that [Secretary of War] Henry Stimson and [Assistant Secretary of War] John McCloy would have made a more careful evaluation of the evacuation proposal than they appear to have done.

nothing but an exclusion order. To cast this case into outlines of racial prejudice, without reference to the real military dangers which were presented, merely confuses the issue. Korematsu was not excluded from the Military Area because of hostility to him or his race. He *was* excluded because we are at war with the Japanese Empire, because the properly constituted military authorities feared an invasion of our West Coast and felt constrained to take proper security measures, because they decided that the military urgency of the situation demanded that all citizens of Japanese ancestry be segregated from the West Coast temporarily, and finally, because Congress, reposing its confidence in this time of war in our military leaders—as inevitably it must—determined that they should have the power to do just this. There was evidence of disloyalty on the part of some, the military authorities considered that the need for action was great, and time was short. We cannot—by availing ourselves of the calm perspective of hindsight—now say that at that time these actions were unjustified.

Korematsu v. United States

Far from the west coast, they would be expected to have a more detached view than the commander on the scene. But here too there seems to have been a tendency to feel that concern for civil liberties was not their responsibility. There is even more of this feeling in Roosevelt's perfunctory approval of the plan in response to a telephone call from Stimson. [Attorney General Francis] Biddle's protests proved to be futile even at the highest levels of government, in part because no significant element of public opinion opposed the relocation. The American Civil Liberties Union, for example, which filed briefs in the

Supreme Court supporting both *Hirabayashi* and *Korematsu* when those cases were argued, was noticeably silent at the time that the program was put into operation.

Once the relocation plan was in place, it could only be challenged in the courts. Was the Supreme Court at fault in upholding first the curfew, in *Hirabayashi,* and then the relocation in *Korematsu?* In *Hirabayashi,* the first case, the Court could have decided the validity of both the relocation requirement and the curfew requirement. The "concurrent sentence" doctrine under which the Court declined to do so is not mandatory but discretionary. But counseling against any broader decision was the well-established rule that the Court should avoid deciding constitutional questions if it is possible to do so. Both the curfew and the relocation program were challenged on constitutional grounds, but the latter was a much more serious infringement of civil liberty than the former. The *Hirabayashi* decision, upholding only the curfew, left the more difficult question of the relocation program for another day.

The *Hirabayashi* Opinion

When that day came—as it did in *Korematsu*—a majority of the Court upheld the relocation program. Justice [Hugo] Black's opinion for the Court in *Korematsu* followed the same line of reasoning as had Chief Justice [Harlan Fiske] Stone's in *Hirabayashi.* But this time there were three dissenters; they had voted to uphold the curfew but voted to strike down the relocation program.

Several criticisms of the Court's opinions in these cases have been made. The most general is of its extremely deferential treatment of the government's argument that the curfew and relocation were necessitated by military considerations. Here one can only echo Justice [Robert H.] Jackson's observation in his dissenting opinion that "in the very nature of things, military decisions are not susceptible of intelligent judicial appraisal." But it surely does not follow from this that a court must therefore invalidate measures based on military judgments. Eugene Rostow suggests the possibility of a judicial inquiry into the entire question of military necessity, but this seems an extraordinarily dubious proposition. Judicial inquiry, with its restrictive rules of evidence, orientation towards resolution of factual disputes in individual cases, and long delays, is ill-suited to determine an issue such as "military necessity." The necessity for prompt action was cogently stated by the Court in its *Hirabayashi* opinion:

> Although the results of the attack on Pearl Harbor were not fully disclosed until much later, it was known that the damage was extensive, and that the Japanese by their successes had gained a naval superiority over our forces in the Pacific which might enable them to seize Pearl Harbor, our largest naval base and the last stronghold of defense lying between Japan and the West Coast. That reasonably prudent men charged with the responsibility of our national defense had ample ground for concluding that they must face the danger of invasion, take measures against it, and in making the choice of measures consider our internal situation, cannot be doubted.

A second criticism is that the decisions in these cases upheld a program that, at bottom, was based on racial distinctions. There are several levels at which this criticism can be made. The broadest is that the Nisei were relocated simply because the Caucasian majority on the west coast (and in the country as a whole) disliked them and wished to remove them as neighbors or as business competitors. The Court's answer to this broad attack seems satisfactory—those of Japanese descent were displaced because of fear that disloyal elements among them would aid Japan in the war. Though there were undoubtedly nativists in California who welcomed a chance to see the Issei and the Nisei removed, it does not follow that this point of view was attributable to the military decision-makers. They, after all, did not at first propose relocation.

But a narrower criticism along the same line has more force to it: the Nisei were evacuated notwithstanding the fact that they were American citizens, and they were treated differently from other Americans. Even in wartime, citizens may not be rounded up and required to prove their loyalty. They may be excluded from sensitive military areas in the absence of a security clearance and may otherwise be denied access to any classified information. But it pushes these propositions to an extreme to say that a sizable geographical area, including the residences of many citizens, may be declared off-limits and the residents required to move. It pushes it to an even greater extreme to say that such persons may be required not only to leave their homes but also to report to and remain in a distant relocation center.

The Court Justifies Relocation

The Supreme Court in its *Hirabayashi* opinion pointed to several facts thought to justify this treatment of the Nisei. Both federal and state restrictions on the rights of Japanese emigrants had prevented their assimilation into the Caucasian population and had intensified their insularity and solidarity. Japanese parents sent their children to Japanese-language schools outside of regular school hours, and there was some evidence that the language schools were a source of Japanese nationalistic propaganda. As many as ten thousand American-born children of Japanese parentage went to Japan for all or part of their education. And even though children born in the United States of Japanese alien parents were U.S. citizens, they were under Japanese law also viewed as citizens of Japan. The Court therefore concluded:

Whatever views we may entertain regarding the loyalty to

this country of the citizens of Japanese ancestry, we cannot reject as unfounded the judgment of the military authorities and of Congress that there were disloyal members of that population, whose number and strength could not be precisely and quickly ascertained. We cannot say that the war-making branches of the Government did not have ground for believing that in a critical hour such persons could not readily be isolated and separately dealt with, and constituted a menace to the national defense and safety, which demanded that prompt and adequate measures be taken to guard against it.

There is considerable irony, of course, in relying on previously existing laws discriminating against Japanese immigrants to conclude that still further disabilities

Because of fear of espionage during World War II, thousands of Japanese Americans were removed from their homes and sent to internment camps. This controversial act was a sore spot of the Roosevelt administration.

should be imposed upon them because they had not been assimilated into the Caucasian majority. But in time of war a nation may be required to respond to a condition without making a careful inquiry as to how that condition came about. . . .

The discrimination against the Nisei lay in the fact that any other citizen could remain in his home unless actually tried and convicted of espionage or sabotage, while the Nisei were removed from their homes without any individualized findings at all. The proffered justification was that attack on or invasion of the west coast by Japan was reasonably feared, and that first-generation American citizens of Japanese descent were more likely than the citizenry as a whole to include potential spies or saboteurs who would assist the enemy.

This view was not totally without support. A "Magic intercept," resulting from the Americans having broken the Japanese code, dated May 1941, contained a message from the Japanese consulate in Los Angeles that "we also have connections with our second-generations working in airplane plants for intelligence purposes." Such information might well have justified exclusion of Nisei, as opposed to other citizens, from work in aircraft factories without strict security clearance, but it falls considerably short of justifying the dislodging of thousands of citizens from their homes on the basis of ancestry. The submissions by the military showed no particular factual inquiry into the likelihood of espionage or sabotage by Nisei, only generalized conclusions that they were "different" from other Americans. But the military has no special expertise in this field, and it should have taken far more substantial findings to justify this sort of discrimination, even in wartime.

The Alien Act of 1798

The Issei, however, who were not citizens, were both by tradition and by law in a quite different category. The legal difference dates back to the Alien Law enacted in 1798, during the administration of President John Adams. Often bracketed together with the Sedition Act passed at the same time, there is a tendency to think that both were repealed as soon as Thomas Jefferson and his Jeffersonian Republicans came to power in 1801. But while the Sedition Act expired under its own terms, the Alien Act, with minor amendments, remained on the books at the time of World War II. It provided:

> Whenever there is a declared war between the United States and any foreign nation or government . . . all natives, citizens, denizens, or subjects of the hostile nation or government, being of the age of fourteen years and upward, who shall be within the United States and not actually naturalized, shall be liable to be apprehended, restrained, secured, and removed as alien enemies. The President is authorized, in any such event, by his proclamation thereof . . . to direct the conduct to be observed, on the part of the United States, toward the aliens who become so liable; the manner and degree of the restraint to which they shall be subjected and in what cases, and upon what security their residence shall be permitted, and to provide for the removal of those who, not being permitted to reside within the United States, refuse or neglect to depart therefrom.

In a case decided shortly after the end of World War II, the Supreme Court, referring to the Alien Law, said:

> Executive power over enemy aliens, undelayed and unhampered by litigation, has been deemed, throughout our history, essential to war-time security. This is in keeping with the practice of the most enlightened of nations and has resulted in treatment of alien enemies more considerate than that which has prevailed among any of our enemies and some of our allies. This statute was enacted or suffered to continue by men who helped

found the Republic and formulate the Bill of Rights, and although it obviously denies enemy aliens the constitutional immunities of citizens, it seems not then to have been supposed that a nation's obligations to its foes could ever be put on a parity with those of its defenders.

The resident enemy alien is constitutionally subject to summary arrest, internment and deportation whenever a "declared war" exists.

Thus, distinctions that might not be permissible between classes of citizens must be viewed otherwise when drawn between classes of aliens.

The Difference Between Germans, Italians and Japanese

The most frequently made charge on behalf of the Issei is that the government treated Japanese enemy aliens differently from enemy aliens of German or Italian citizenship, when we were at war with all three countries. It appears that there was some removal of Italian enemy aliens along the west coast for a brief period of time. But there seems little doubt that the west coast Issei were treated quite differently from the majority of German or Italian nationals residing in this country. It should be pointed out, however, that there do not appear to have been the same concentrations of German or Italian nationals along the west coast in areas near major defense plants. Japanese emigration to the United States had occurred entirely within the preceding half-century, and the emigrants resided almost entirely on the west coast; Italian emigration had taken place over a considerably longer period of time, and German emigration had gone on since colonial days. People of German and Italian ancestry were far more spread out in the population in general than were the Issei. While there were areas of German or Italian concentration on the eastern seaboard, the danger feared there was not attacks from

German bombers or invasion of German troops, but the sinking of Allied merchant ships by German submarines.

On the west coast, on the other hand, there was the very real fear of attack by Japanese bombers flying from aircraft carriers, if not actual invasion by Japanese ground forces. As noted before, these fears were all but groundless after the Battle of Midway in June 1942, but the relocation program was established and put into effect before that decisive encounter. And as Chief Justice Stone pointed out in *Hirabayashi,* United States aircraft production was highly concentrated on the west coast. The capacity of those plants might have been greatly reduced by a successful air raid, and there is some evidence that residents of Japanese ancestry, loyal to Japan, had been placed in the aircraft plants.

These distinctions seem insufficient to justify such a sharp difference of treatment between Japanese and German and Italian aliens in peacetime. But they do seem legally adequate to support the difference in treatment between the two classes of enemy aliens in time of war.

Japanese Americans Did Not Pose a Threat to American Security

Michi Weglyn

In 1941, with all signs pointing toward imminent war with Japan, Curtis B. Munson, at the behest of President Roosevelt and the State Department, carried out a study of the degree of loyalty found among American residents of Japanese descent in October of 1941. Munson's findings indicated that an overwhelming majority of Japanese Americans—those who emigrated from Japan as well as those born in the United States—were extremely loyal to their adopted homeland.

In the following essay, Michi Weglyn writes that the forced evacuation of Japanese Americans from California, Oregon and Washington had nothing to do with the security risk Japanese Americans may have posed, as many government officials claimed. Instead, writes Weglyn, the relocation of 100,000 Japanese Americans was the result of rampant anti-Asian hysteria on the west coast. Michi Weglyn is the author of *Years of Infamy: The Untold Story of America's Concentration Camps*, from which the following essay is excerpted.

B Y FALL OF 1941, WAR WITH JAPAN APPEARED IMMINENT. For well over a year, coded messages going in and out of Tokyo had been intercepted and decoded by Washington cryptoanalysts. With relations between Tokyo and Washington rapidly deteriorating, a desperate sense of national

Excerpted from *Years of Infamy: The Untold Story of America's Concentration Camps*, by Michi Weglyn (New York: Morrow Quill, 1976). Copyright ©1976 by Michi Nishiura Weglyn. Reprinted by permission of the California State Polytechnic University, Pomona.

urgency was evidenced in messages to Ambassador Nomura, then carrying on negotiations in the nation's capital. On July 25, Japan had seized south French Indo-China. The activation the following day of the Morgenthau-Stimson plan, calling for the complete cessation of trade with Japan and the freezing of her assets in America—Great Britain and the Netherlands following suit—had resulted in the strangulation and near collapse of the island economy.

By late September, Tokyo's coded messages included demands for data concerning the Pacific Fleet stationed at Pearl Harbor. Of great implication for U.S. Army and Naval Intelligence was the September 24 dispatch directed to Consul Nagao Kita in Honolulu:

HENCEFORTH, WE WOULD LIKE TO HAVE YOU MAKE REPORTS CONCERNING VESSELS ALONG THE FOLLOWING LINES IN SO FAR AS POSSIBLE:

1. THE WATERS OF PEARL HARBOR ARE TO BE DIVIDED ROUGHLY INTO FIVE SUB-AREAS. WE HAVE NO OBJECTION TO YOUR ABBREVIATING AS MUCH AS YOU LIKE. AREA A. WATERS BETWEEN FORD ISLAND AND THE ARSENAL. AREA B. WATERS ADJACENT TO THE ISLAND SOUTH AND WEST OF FORD ISLAND. THIS AREA IS ON THE OPPOSITE SIDE OF THE ISLAND FROM AREA A. AREA C. EAST LOCH. AREA D. MIDDLE LOCH. AREA E. WEST LOCH AND THE COMMUNICATING WATER ROUTES.

2. WITH REGARD TO WARSHIPS AND AIRCRAFT CARRIERS WE WOULD LIKE TO HAVE YOU REPORT ON THOSE AT ANCHOR (THESE ARE NOT SO IMPORTANT), TIED UP AT WHARVES, BUOYS, AND IN DOCK. DESIGNATE TYPES AND CLASSES BRIEFLY. IF POSSIBLE, WE WOULD LIKE TO HAVE YOU MAKE MENTION OF THE FACT WHEN THERE ARE TWO OR MORE VESSELS ALONGSIDE THE SAME WHARF.

With all signs pointing to a rapid approach of war and the Hawaiian naval outpost the probable target, a highly secret intelligence-gathering was immediately ordered by the President. Mandated with *pro forma* investigative powers as a Special Representative of the State Department was one Curtis B. Munson. His mission: to get as precise a picture as possible of the degree of loyalty to be found among residents of Japanese descent, both on the West Coast of the United States and in Hawaii.

Carried out in the month of October and the first weeks of November, Munson's investigation resulted in a twenty-five-page report of uncommon significance, especially as it served to corroborate data representing more than a decade of prodigious snooping and spying by the various U.S. intelligence services, both domestic and military. *It certified a remarkable, even extraordinary degree of loyalty among this generally suspect ethnic group. . . .*

On February 5, 1942, a week before the go-ahead decision for the evacuation was handed down, Stimson informed the Chief Executive in a letter sent along with the President's personal copy of the Munson Report: "In response to your memorandum of November 8, the Department gave careful study and consideration to the matters reported by Mr. C.B. Munson in his memorandum covering the Japanese situation on the West Coast." This meant that the General Staff had had fully three months to study, circulate, review, and analyze the contents of the report before it was returned to the President.

Owing to the wartime concealment of this important document, few, if any, realized how totally distorted was the known truth in pro-internment hysterics emanating from the military, with the exception of those in naval intelligence and the FBI, whose surveillance of the Japanese minority over the years had been exhaustive. Both services, to their credit, are on record as having opposed the President's decision for evacuation.

To the average American the evacuation tragedy, well shrouded as it remains in tidied-up historical orthodoxy and in the mythology spawned by the "total-war" frenzy, remains no more than a curious aberration in American history. Only during the civil rights turbulence of the sixties, when personal liberties of unpopular minorities were once again in jeopardy, was interest sharply rekindled in this blurred-out episode in America's past. A generation of the nation's youth, who had grown up knowing nothing or little of so colossal a national scandal as American-style concentration camps, suddenly demanded to know what it was that had happened. Noticed also was an upsurge of interest among the "Sansei" (the children of the second-generation "Nisei [Japanese Americans born in the United States]"), some of whom had been born in these camps, who now wanted to be told everything that their parents and grandparents, the "Issei [immigrants from Japan]," had tried so hard to forget.

Yet the enormity of this incredible governmental hoax cannot begin to be fathomed without taking into consideration the definitive loyalty findings of Curtis B. Munson, especially in relation to the rationale that in 1942 "justified" the sending of some 110,000 men, women, and children to concentration camps: namely, that an "unknown" number of Japanese Americans presented a potential threat of dire fifth-column peril to the national security, that it would be difficult to sort out the dangerous ones in so short a time, so to play it safe all should be locked up.

Anti-Asian Feelings

Behind it all was a half century of focusing anti-Asian hates on the Japanese minority by West Coast pressure groups resentful of them as being hyperefficient competitors. An inordinate amount of regional anxiety had also accompanied Japan's rapid rise to power. Years of media-abetted conditioning to the possibility of war, invasion, and conquest by waves and waves of fanatic, Emperor-worshiping yellow men—invariably aided by harmless-seeming Japanese gardeners and fisherfolk who were really spies and saboteurs in disguise—had evoked a latent paranoia as the news from the Pacific in the early weeks of the war brought only reports of cataclysmic Allied defeats.

In 1941, the number of Japanese Americans living in the continental United States totaled 127,000. Over 112,000 of them lived in the three Pacific Coast states of Oregon, Washington, and California. Of this group, nearly 80 percent of the total (93,000) resided in the state of California alone.

Japanese-American school children in San Francisco recite the pledge of allegiance to the American flag. After the Japanese attack on Pearl Harbor the large Japanese-American population on the west coast fell suspect to espionage rumors.

In the hyperactive minds of longtime residents of California, where antipathy toward Asians was the most intense, the very nature of the Pearl Harbor attack provided ample—and prophetic—proof of inherent Japanese treachery. As the Imperial Army chalked up success after success on the far-flung Pacific front, and as rumors of prowling enemy submarines proliferated wildly, the West Coast atmosphere became charged with a panicky fear of impending invasion and a profound suspicion that Japanese Americans in their midst were organized for coordinated subversive activity. For the myriad anti-Oriental forces and influential agriculturists who had long cast their covetous eyes over the coastal webwork of rich Japanese-owned land, a superb opportunity had thus become theirs for the long-sought expulsion of an unwanted minority. . . .

A "Second Pearl Harbor"?

Then, with the wild tales of resident Japanese perfidy that Pearl Harbor unleashed, rumors flew back and forth that Issei landowners had settled in stealth and with diabolical intent near vital installations. Their purpose: a "second Pearl Harbor." At the Tolan Committee hearings, then ostensibly weighing the pros and cons of evacuation, impressive documentation was unfurled by the top law officer of California, Attorney General Earl Warren (later to become the Chief Justice of the U.S. Supreme Court), purporting to support his theory of a possible insurrection in the making: that, with malice aforethought, Japanese Americans had "infiltrated themselves into every strategic spot in our coastal and valley counties.". . .

There was no possible way of separating the loyal from the disloyal, insisted the Attorney General: ". . . when we are dealing with the Caucasian race we have methods that will test the loyalty of them . . . But when we deal with the Japanese we are in an entirely different field and we cannot form any opinion that we believe to be sound." Warren urged speedy removal.

Unfortunately for the Nisei and Issei, it was an election year. The tide of "public opinion"—the ferocity of the clamor, at least—indicated total unconditional removal, citizen or not. And all politicians were falling in line. . . .

In striking contradiction to such insinuations and untruths fabricated of prejudice, a far kindlier assessment of

Issei and Nisei acculturation, aspirations, and value priorities had been documented for the President in the weeks prior to the outbreak of hostilities. Munson's prewar assessment had been strongly positive; his commendation of the Nisei was glowing:

> Their family life is disciplined and honorable. The children are obedient and the girls virtuous. . . .

> There are still Japanese in the United States who will tie dynamite around their waist and make a human bomb out of themselves. We grant this, but today they are few. Many things indicate that very many joints in the Japanese set-up show age, and many elements are not what they used to be. The weakest from a Japanese standpoint are the Nisei. They are universally estimated from 90 to 98 percent loyal to the United States if the Japanese-educated element of the Kibei is excluded. The Nisei are pathetically eager to show this loyalty. They are not Japanese in culture. They are foreigners to Japan. Though American citizens they are not accepted by Americans, largely because they look differently [sic] and can be easily recognized. The Japanese American Citizens League should be encouraged, the while an eye is kept open, to see that Tokio does not get its finger in this pie—which it has in a few cases attempted to do. The loyal Nisei hardly knows where to turn. Some gesture of protection or wholehearted acceptance of this group would go a long way to swinging them away from any last romantic hankering after old Japan. They are not oriental or mysterious, they are very American and are of a proud, self-respecting race suffering from a little inferiority complex and a lack of contact with the white boys they went to school with. They are eager for this contact and to work alongside them. . . .

The Loyalty of the Issei

Contradicting widely held assumptions to the contrary, Munson's following assessment of the immigrant group reveals the personal esteem in which many Issei had been held as individuals, even in the face of mounting prewar feelings:

> The Issei, or first generation, is considerably weakened in their loyalty to Japan by the fact that they have chosen to make this their home and have brought up their children here. They expect to die here. They are quite fearful of being put in a concentration camp. Many would take out American citizenship if allowed to do so. The haste of this report does not allow us to go into this more fully. The Issei have to break with their religion, their god and Emperor, their family, their ancestors and their after-life in order to be loyal to the United States. They are also still legally Japanese. Yet they do break, and send their boys off to the Army with pride and tears. They are good neighbors. They are old men fifty-five to sixty-five, for the most part simple and dignified. Roughly they were Japanese lower middle class, about analogous to the pilgrim fathers. . . .

The report continued: "Now that we have roughly given a background and a description of the Japanese elements in the United States, the question naturally arises— what will these people do in case of a war between the United States and Japan?" In other words, could Japanese Americans be trusted to withstand the ties of "blood" and "race" in the ultimate test of loyalty, of being pitted against their own kind? Would there be the *banzai* uprisings, the espionage and sabotage long prophesied and propagandized by anti-Oriental hate exploiters? "As interview after interview piled up," reported Investigator Munson, "those bringing in results began to call it the same old tune."

> The story was all the same. There is no Japanese "problem" on the Coast. There will be no armed uprising of Japanese. There will undoubtedly be some sabotage financed by Japan and executed largely by imported agents . . . In each Naval District there are about 250 to

300 suspects under surveillance. It is easy to get on the suspect list, merely a speech in favor of Japan at some banquet being sufficient to land one there. The Intelligence Services are generous with the title of suspect and are taking no chances. Privately, they believe that only 50 or 60 in each district can be classed as really dangerous. The Japanese are hampered as saboteurs because of their easily recognized physical appearance. It will be hard for them to get near anything to blow up *if it is guarded.* There is far more danger from Communists and people of the Bridges type on the Coast than there is from Japanese. The Japanese here is almost exclusively a farmer, a fisherman or a small businessman. He has no entree to plants or intricate machinery.

. . . The wartime suppression of the Munson papers, like the more familiar Pentagon Papers, once again makes evident how executive officers of the Republic are able to mislead public opinion by keeping hidden facts which are precisely the opposite of what the public is told—information vital to the opinions they hold.

In the case of Japanese Americans, data regarding their character and integrity were positive and "exceedingly uniform," the facts clear cut. But as once observed by Nobel Peace Prize recipient Sir Norman Angell: "Men, particularly in political matters, are not guided by the facts but by their opinions about the facts." Under the guise of an emergency and pretended threats to the national security, the citizenry was denied the known facts, public opinion skillfully manipulated, and a cruel and massive governmental hoax enacted. According to one of the foremost authorities on constitutional law, Dr. Eugene V. Rostow: "One hundred thousand persons were sent to concentration camps on a record which wouldn't support a conviction for stealing a dog."

Roosevelt Did Not Do Enough for Jewish Refugees

Arthur D. Morse

Though President Herbert Hoover enacted the harsh immigration statutes of the 1930s, President Roosevelt did nothing to relax the stringent measures to accommodate the growing number of refugees from Nazi-dominated Europe. Even as the Nazis burned synagogues, smashed the windows of Jewish-owned shops, and herded thousands of Jews into concentration camps, Roosevelt insisted upon adhering to the letter of American immigration law, thus assuring that only a trickle of refugees found asylum in the United States. In the following essay, award-winning journalist Arthur D. Morse writes that in spite of the unprecedented circumstances facing the Jews of Europe, American immigration laws were constricted further, thus ensuring that the already low quotas were not met.

I N 1933, WITH THE TOTAL U.S. IMMIGRATION QUOTA FIXED at 153,774, only 23,068 newcomers arrived; of these, a mere 1,798 were Germans. In 1934, in spite of the intensity of the Nazi persecution, only 4,716 Germans entered the United States, and in 1935 the number increased slightly, to 5,117. Between 1933 and 1935, about one-third of the German immigrants were Jewish. From 1933 to 1936 more Germans departed from the United States than entered it. The total population of the United States remained quite

Excerpted from the book *While Six Million Died*, by Arthur D. Morse. Copyright ©1967 by Arthur D. Morse. Published by The Overlook Press, 1 Overlook Dr., Woodstock, NY 12498. Reprinted with permission.

constant during the years preceding World War II which many Americans associate with wide-scale immigration.

As a matter of fact, during the entire Hitler period the number of immigrants lagged far behind the total permitted under U.S. law. From 1933 to 1943, there were 1,244,858 unfilled places on U.S. immigration quotas. Of these vacancies, 341,567 had been allotted to citizens of countries dominated or occupied by Germany or her allies. Each unfilled place represented a potential life exposed to annihilation.

America's Legacy?

What had happened to George Washington's admonition to his countrymen "humbly and fervently to beseech the kind Author of these blessings . . . to render this country more and more a safe and propitious asylum for the unfortunates of other countries"?

And what of the legacy of Thomas Jefferson, who, in 1801, had asked: "Shall we refuse the unhappy fugitives from distress that hospitality which the savages of the wilderness extended to our forefathers arriving in this land? Shall oppressed humanity find no asylum on this globe?"

The barriers that faced the refugees from Hitler were erected late in the nineteenth century. Before that time the image of America as a haven had gained luster as the refugees who fled the poverty, persecution and exploitation of the Old World were welcomed into the New. Until the 1890's the nations of western and northern Europe— Great Britain and Ireland; Germany; Norway, Sweden and Denmark—yielded the overwhelming majority of immigrants. These countries provided 72 percent of the new arrivals between 1881 and 1890, while only 18.3 percent came from southern and eastern Europe.

The northern and western Europeans were, for the most part, industrious farmers and skilled workers. The Irish tended to concentrate in the East, but there was a large westward movement of other immigrants. These were predominantly Protestant, with a high literacy rate, and they were easily assimilated into the existing population.

The Geographic Pattern Changes

At the turn of the century the geographic pattern was reversed. Millions of immigrants poured in from the destitute countries of southern and eastern Europe. Between 1901 and 1910, more than 70 percent of the immigrants were Poles, Russians, Austrians, Hungarians, Italians, Rumanians, Czechs, Slovaks, Serbs and Croats. Large-scale migration from the United Kingdom, Germany and Scandinavia had ended.

These new immigrants were mainly Catholic, Greek Orthodox or Jewish. They were desperately poor, and their proportion of illiteracy was higher than among their pre-

Jewish immigrants searching for refuge from the Nazis turned hopeful eyes to America. Yet due to various immigration laws the number of Jews to actually achieve asylum in America was few.

decessors. Unlike most of the earlier immigrants, who had dispersed throughout the nation, they settled in the cities. They remained in identifiable groups, retained much of their language and customs, and became easy prey for exploitation by landlords and factory owners. Moreover, the large reservoir of unskilled workers alarmed the labor organizations, the burgeoning "foreign" slums appalled the city dwellers, and the cacophony of unfamiliar sounds disturbed the "earlier" Americans. The drive to restrict immigration gained momentum and was aided by laws passed in the late 1800's. The restrictions against immigrants likely to become public charges, a stipulation which would later be applied to large numbers of Jews fleeing Hitler, was first enunciated in 1882. The immigration act of that year excluded "any convict, lunatic, idiot or any other person unable to take care of himself or herself without becoming a public charge."

The Alien Contract Labor Law of 1885 would also be invoked in the Hitler era, although it was designed for an utterly different purpose—the prevention of such abuses as the importation of foreign labor to drive down wage rates, particularly in the coal fields. The act stipulated that it was unlawful to assist the entry of aliens under a prior contract for labor. . . .

The Depression Alters American Immigration Policy

Until September 1930 the provision denying admission to an immigrant "likely to become a public charge" had rarely been invoked; immigrants of good character and robust health, and with perhaps $100, were regarded as good risks in the expanding American economy. It was the massive unemployment in the wake of the 1929 crash and not refugees from Adolf Hitler which caused the "public charge" provision to be resurrected from the statute books, dusted off and utilized. And it was Herbert Hoover, not

Franklin D. Roosevelt, who revived it.

President Hoover issued a White House statement on September 8, 1930, calling attention to the abnormal times and announcing that consular officers "will before issuing a visa have to pass judgment with particular care on whether the applicant may become a public charge, and if the applicant cannot convince the officer that it is not probable, the visa will be refused."

The President made it clear that if the consul believed that the applicant might become a public charge *at any time,* even long after his arrival, the consul must refuse the visa. The State Department obeyed these instructions diligently, and the number of aliens admitted to the United States fell from 241,700 in 1930 to 97,139 in 1931. Immigration further plummeted to 35,576 in 1932, the year before Hitler came to power. . . .

Another major obstacle to immigration for Jews fleeing from Hitler concerned Section 7 (c) of the Immigration Act of 1924, which required the applicant to furnish a police certificate of good character for the previous five years, together with a record of military service, two certified copies of a birth certificate and "two copies of all other available public records" kept by the authorities in the country from which he was departing. The law required these documents only "if available," but many American consuls insisted upon full dossiers—and the police certificate in particular.

Although the notion of a Jew dropping by police headquarters to receive a certificate of good character from his oppressors may strike the reader as a particularly sardonic touch of bureaucracy, State Department files refer repeatedly to this requirement and its importance. . . .

As if the "public charge" provision, the necessity to supply police records and the complexities of the "contract labor" clause were not enough, a further restriction in the Immigration Act of 1917 called for the "exclusion of persons whose ticket or passage is paid by any corporation, association or society, municipality or foreign government, either directly or indirectly." The originators of this provision could not have foreseen the plight of the German Jews, who were stripped of all their possessions before being cast adrift on endless seas. They were expected to be self-sufficient though penniless, capable of supporting themselves though unemployed, and prepared to pay their passage without accepting help from friends.

But the Immigration Act was not revised. Everyone from the White House on down expressed fears that any attempts to reform it would bring down the wrath of the conservative Southerners, who dominated congressional committees and who would be just as happy to end immigration altogether as to simplify its procedures. Martin Dies of Texas, who led the restrictionists in the House of Representatives, put it simply: "We must ignore the tears of sobbing sentimentalists and internationalists, and we must permanently close, lock and bar the gates of our country to new immigration waves and then throw the keys away." . . .

Financial Pressures Mount

As Germany tightened the noose, the financial pressures against Jewish emigrants became more severe. At the beginning of Hitler's regime, Jews who left Germany were permitted to take out as much as $10,000, but soon this was reduced to $6,000. When it was lowered to $4,000, the American consul in Stuttgart reported that the reduction "will result in many immigrants to the United States from Germany encountering grave difficulty in showing that they are not excludable under the public charge clause."

But the Nazis had only started their campaign to plunder the Jews, and soon the maximum amount they could take with them dropped to $800. In October 1934 the Third Reich issued its most drastic currency restriction, limiting each emigrant to a total of 10 reichsmarks (about

$4). The Jews were thus trapped by both German and American regulations.

The harshness of American immigration policy was not lost on Hitler, who turned each aspect of the world's apathy into a weapon for himself. A month after he had assumed power he issued a statement that American citizens had no right to protest his anti-Semitism in view of the United States' own racial discrimination in its immigration policies. "Through its immigration law," said Hitler, "America has inhibited the unwelcome influx of such races as it has been unable to tolerate in its midst. Nor is America now ready to open its doors to Jews fleeing from Germany." . . .

Attempts to Loosen Rigid Policies

There had been many attempts by prominent Americans to make the Roosevelt Administration relax the rigid implementation of the "public charge" and other restrictions which had reduced immigration to a trickle.

The American Civil Liberties Union made a determined effort on September 10, 1933, addressing an appeal to the President signed by thirty-six distinguished educators, lawyers and clergymen, including Reinhold Niebuhr, Professor Felix Frankfurter, the Reverend John Haynes Holmes, Oswald Garrison Villard, Professor Charles A. Beard and the Misses Jane Addams and Lillian Wald. They called for "revision of the immigration laws to admit religious and political refugees, particularly from Germany, in harmony with the American tradition of asylum for refugees escaping from foreign tyrannies."

Several specific recommendations were submitted to the President. The first one called for the posting of bonds by responsible citizens, as insurance that the immigrants would not become public charges. Next, they urged him to revise President Hoover's executive order of 1930, which, they said, "had the effect practically of stopping all immigration." Third, they suggested that consuls accept certificates of good character in behalf of the immigrants instead of requiring police certificates from the countries they were fleeing. Finally, they asked the President "to call to the attention of Consuls the special claims in law of political and religious refugees to asylum in the United States.". . .

There was but one significant response to complaints about the harsh implementation of the immigration law. Cordell Hull notified consuls to be lenient to applicants who might be endangered by efforts to obtain a police certificate.

Living to the Letter of Immigration Law

Throughout the prewar and wartime years Franklin D. Roosevelt insisted on living up to the letter of the immigration law, maintaining that restrictionist elements in Congress would block any reform. But a change in the law would not have been necessary. As James McDonald, a specialist in international affairs who had been chairman of the Foreign Policy Association, observed: "Just as President Hoover, by administrative interpretation, in effect instructed the consuls to block immigration, so now President Roosevelt could, by relaxing further the requirements in the case of refugees, make easier the admission of a few thousand additional Germans a year."

But there would be no relaxation. In 1938 the Nazis burned every synagogue in the nation, shattered the windows of every Jewish establishment, hauled twenty-five thousand innocent people to concentration camps, and fined the Jews 1,000,000,000 marks for the damage.

Five days later, at a White House press conference, a reporter asked the President, "Would you recommend a relaxation of our immigration restrictions so that the Jewish refugees could be received in this country?"

"That is not in contemplation," replied the President. "We have the quota system."

The United States not only insisted upon its immigration law throughout the Nazi era, but administered it with severity and callousness.

In spite of unprecedented circumstances, the law was constricted so that even its narrow quotas were not met.

The lamp remained lifted beside the golden door, but the flame had been extinguished and the door was padlocked.

Roosevelt Did All He Could for Europe's Jews

WILLIAM J. VANDEN HEUVEL

Charges that President Roosevelt did not do enough for Jewish victims of Nazi tyranny have no basis in fact, argues William J. vanden Heuvel, president of the Franklin and Eleanor Roosevelt Institute. When Hitler and the Nazis came to power in 1933, Roosevelt recognized the evils of Nazism and was very vocal in condemning the Jewish persecution. In the following essay, adapted from his speech at the fifth Franklin and Eleanor Roosevelt Distinguished Lecture on October 17, 1996, vanden Heuvel points out that President Roosevelt—facing an isolationist Congress with a powerful anti-immigration contingent—accepted twice as many Jewish refugees as all other countries combined. Though Congress would not let Roosevelt raise the quota of Jewish refugees allowed into the United States, the president worked tirelessly to find safe havens elsewhere. In addition to creating the War Refugee Board, which attempted to relocate those fleeing from the Nazis once World War II started, President Roosevelt put constant pressure on European allies to accept as many refugees as possible.

FIVE WEEKS AFTER ADOLF HITLER BECAME CHANCELLOR of Germany in 1933, Franklin Roosevelt became President of the United States. Roosevelt's loathing of the whole Nazi regime was known the moment he took office. Alone

---

Excerpted from "America, Franklin D. Roosevelt, and the Holocaust," by William J. vanden Heuvel, keynote address of the fifth annual Franklin and Eleanor Roosevelt Distinguished Lecture, Roosevelt University, Chicago, Illinois, October 17, 1996. Entire text available at www.newdeal.feri.org/feri/wvh.htm. Reprinted with permission from the author.

among the leaders of the world, he stood in opposition to Hitler from the very beginning. In a book published in 1937, Winston Churchill—to whom free humanity everywhere must be eternally indebted and without whose courage and strength the defeat of Nazi Germany could never have been achieved—described Hitler's treatment of the Jews, stating that "concentration camps pock-mark the German soil . . ." and concluding his essay by writing that "the world lives on hopes that the worst is over and that we may live to see Hitler a gentler figure in a happier age." Roosevelt had no such hopes. He never wavered in his belief that the pagan malignancy of Hitler and his followers had to be destroyed. Thomas Mann, the most famous of the non-Jewish refugees from the Nazis, met with FDR at the White House in 1935 and confided that for the first time he believed the Nazis would be beaten because in Roosevelt he had met someone who truly understood the evil of Adolf Hitler. . . .

The Roosevelts' Efforts to Aid Refugees

The President and Mrs. Roosevelt were leaders in the effort to help the German Jews fleeing political persecution. Mrs. Roosevelt was a founder of the International Rescue Committee in 1933 which brought intellectuals, labor leaders, and political figures fleeing Hitler to sanctuary in the United States. President Roosevelt made a public point of inviting many of them to the White House. In 1936, in response to the Nazi confiscation of personal assets as a precondition to Jewish emigration, Roosevelt greatly modified Hoover's ruling regarding financial sponsorship for refugees thereby allowing a substantially greater number of visas to be issued. As a result, the United States accepted twice as many Jewish refugees than did the rest of the world put together. As [historian] Professor [Gerhard] Weinberg has stated, Roosevelt acted in the face of strong and politically damaging criticism for what was generally considered a pro-Jewish attitude by him personally and by his Administration.

Hitler's policy never wavered in trying to force the Jews to leave Germany. After the Anschluss [the expansion of Germany to its pre–World War I boundaries] in Austria, Roosevelt, on March 25, 1938, called an international conference on the refugee crisis. Austria's 185,000 Jews were now in jeopardy. The conference met in Evian, France. There was no political advantage for Roosevelt in calling for a conference "to facilitate the emigration from Germany and Austria of political refugees." No other major political leader in any country matched his concern and involvement. The Evian Conference tried to open new doors in the western hemisphere. The Dominican Republic, for example, offered sanctuary to 100,000 refugees. The Inter-Governmental Committee (IGC) was established, hopefully to pressure the Germans to allow the Jews to leave with enough resources to begin their new lives. The devastating blow at Evian was the message from the Polish and Romanian governments that they expected the same right as the Germans to expel their Jewish populations. There were less than 475,000 German and Austrian Jews at this point—a number manageable in an emigration plan that the 29 participating nations could prepare, but with the possibility of 3.5 million more from eastern Europe, the concern now was that any offer of help would only encourage authoritarian governments to brutalize any unwanted portion of their populations, expecting their criminal acts against their own citizens to force the democracies to give them haven. The German emigration problem was manageable. Forced emigration from eastern Europe was not. The Nazi genocide was in the future—and unimaginable to the Jews and probably at the time unimagined by the Nazis. National attitudes then are not very different than today's. No country allows any and every refugee to enter without limitations. Quotas are thought even now to deter unscrupulous and impoverished regimes from forcing their unwanted people on other countries.

Kristallnacht

By the end of 1938, *Kristallnacht* had happened. Its impact on the Jews of Germany and Austria was overwhelming. Munich was a tragic reality. Truncated Czechoslovakia would last six months before Hitler broke his promise and occupied the rest of the country. The German Jew at last understood the barbarism of the Nazis—and that Hitler was totally in power. America's reaction to *Kristallnacht* was stronger than any of the democracies'. Roosevelt recalled his ambassador from Germany. For the first time since the First World War an American president had summoned home an ambassador to a major power under such circumstances. At his press conference then, Roosevelt said: "I myself can scarcely believe that such things could occur in a twentieth-century civilization." He extended the visitors' visas of all Germans and Austrians in the United States who felt threatened. The reaction of Americans in opinion polls showed overwhelming anger and disgust with the Nazis and sympathy for the Jews. Roosevelt remained the target of the hardcore anti-Semites in America. He welcomed them as enemies and in brilliant maneuvering, he isolated them from mainstream America and essentially equated their anti-Semitism with treason and the destruction of both the national interest and national defense. Recognizing the inertia, frequent hostility, and sometime anti-Semitism in the State Department, he entrusted Sumner Welles, the Undersecretary of State and a person totally sympathetic to Jewish needs, to be his instrument of action. President Kennedy, a generation later, commented to friends that he would order something to happen at the State Department—and frequently nothing would happen. Roosevelt understood as Kennedy and every President learns that there is a bureaucracy in government that can limit the possibilities of executive action.

Immigration procedures were complicated and sometimes harshly administered. The immigration laws and quotas were jealously guarded by Congress, supported by a strong, broad cross-section of Americans who were against all immigrants, not alone Jews. Of course, there were racists and anti-Semites in the Congress and in the country— there are today—only now, after sixty years of government based on liberal values, they dare not speak their true attitudes. The State Department, which jealously guarded its administrative authority in the granting of visas, was frequently more concerned with Congressional attitudes and criticisms than in reflecting American decency and generosity in helping people increasingly in despair and panic. Roosevelt undoubtedly made a mistake in appointing . . . Breckenridge Long as Assistant Secretary of State. Many allege Long was an anti-Semite. Others argue "that he was in an impossible situation with an insurmountable task." His presence at State was undoubtedly an assurance to the Congress that the immigration laws would be strictly enforced. On the other hand there were countless Foreign Service officers who did everything possible to help persecuted, innocent people—just as they would today. There was an attitude that there were many sanctuaries available in the world besides the United States, so the Department, controlled by an elite and very conservative officialdom, was quite prepared to make Congressional attitudes the guide for their administration of immigration procedures rather than the attitudes of the White House. Congress looked at the turmoil in Germany as a European problem in which it did not want America to be involved. Nevertheless, between 1933 and 1941, 35 percent of all immigrants to America under quota guidelines were Jewish. After *Kristallnacht*, Jewish immigrants were more than one-half of all immigrants admitted to the United States. Of course, there were other countries of refuge—many of them preferred by German Jews who—like everyone else did not foresee the Nazi madness of conquest and extermination—

and who wanted to stay in Europe. Public opinion everywhere in the democracies was repelled by the Nazi persecution. Great Britain, for example, after *Kristallnacht* granted immigration visas essentially without limit. In the first six months of 1939, 91,780 German and Austrian Jews were admitted to England, often as a temporary port en route to the Dominions or other parts of the Empire.

Roosevelt from the beginning saw the larger threat of the Nazis. Hitler wanted to present Germany as the champion of a universal struggle against the Jews. Roosevelt would not let him. The President understood that he had to explain the vital interest that all Americans had in stopping Hitler in terms of their own security, at the same time protecting Jews from being isolated as the sole cause of the inevitable confrontation. He pressured the Europeans to respond to Hitler. His speech in 1937 calling for the quarantine of the aggressors was met with political hostility at home and abroad. He was constantly seeking havens for the refugees in other countries knowing that he did not have the power to change the quota system of our own country. His critics refuse to acknowledge limitations on presidential power but clearly the President could not unilaterally command an increase in quotas. In fact, his Congressional leaders, including Representative Dickstein who chaired the House subcommittee on immigration, warned him that reactionary forces in the Congress might well use any attempt to increase the quotas as an opportunity to reduce them. Faulting FDR for not using his political power to urge changes in immigration laws when he knew he could not win—or worse, that the isolationists would work to reduce the quotas, does not make much sense. . . .

It is important to say over and over again that it was a time and a place when no one foresaw the events that became the Holocaust. Given the reality of the Holocaust, all of us in every country—and certainly in America—can only wish that we would have done more, that our immigration barriers had been less, that our Congress had had a broader world view, that every public servant had reflected the attitudes of Franklin and Eleanor Roosevelt. . . . Nevertheless, the United States—a nation remote from the world in a way our children can hardly understand—accepted twice as many Jewish refugees than did the rest of the world put together.

The "Voyage of the Damned"

Among the events that cause despair and anguish when we read about it is the fate of the ship, the *St. Louis* of the Hamburg-America line which left Germany and arrived in Cuba on May 27, 1939, with 936 passengers, 930 of them Jewish refugees. This was three months before the outbreak of the war, and three years before the establishment of the death camps. Other ships had made the same journey, and their passengers disembarked successfully, but on May 5 the Cuban government had issued a decree curtailing the power of the corrupt director general of immigration to issue landing certificates. The new regulations requiring $500 bonds from each approved immigrant had been transmitted to the shipping line but only 22 passengers of the *St. Louis* had fulfilled the requirements before leaving Hamburg on May 13. The 22 were allowed to land but intense negotiations with the Cuban government regarding the other passengers—negotiations in which American Jewish agencies participated—broke down despite pressure from our government. It was not an unreported event. Tremendous international attention focused on the *St. Louis*, later made famous as the "Voyage of the Damned." Secretary of State Cordell Hull, Secretary of the Treasury Henry Morgenthau, Jr., and others, including Eleanor Roosevelt, worked to avoid the harsh reality of the immigration laws, for example, by attempting to land the passengers as "tourists" in the Virgin Islands. Despite the legal inability of the United States to accept the passengers of the *St. Louis* as immigrants, our diplomats were significantly helpful in resettling them. None—not one—of the passengers of the *St. Louis* were returned to Nazi Germany. They were all resettled in democratic countries—288 in the United Kingdom, the rest in France, the Netherlands, Belgium and Denmark. The Nazi genocide was in the future, unforeseen and unimaginable by the Jews and those who wanted to help them. . . .

The Proposal to Bomb Auschwitz

The proposal to bomb Auschwitz has become the symbol of American indifference and complicity in the Holocaust. The War Department's rejection of this proposal on the ground that it would divert air support from the war effort was, according to David Wyman, the author of *The Abandonment of the Jews,* merely an excuse. "The real reason," Professor Wyman writes, was that "to the American military, Europe's Jews represented an extraneous problem and an unwanted burden." Is there any doubt as to what [Chief of Staff] George Marshall or Dwight Eisenhower would say to that indictment of America and its armed forces? For America's Jews today, I find there is nothing that disturbs them more, that causes them to question Jewish admiration of FDR more, that permits them to accept the judgment that America's passivity and anti-Semitism makes us complicitous in history's worst crime than the so-called refusal to bomb Auschwitz. Nothing is more important therefore than to review the facts.

The polemicists would have us believe that many American Jewish groups petitioned our government to bomb Auschwitz. That allegation is thoroughly wrong and discredited. The focal center of the Holocaust Museum's exhibit on bombing Auschwitz is a letter from Leon Kubowitzki, head of the Rescue Department of the World Jewish Congress, in which he forwarded, without endorsement, a request from the Czech State Council (in exile in

Roosevelt's Hands Are Tied

In his book Roosevelt Confronts Hitler: America's Entry into World War II, *author Patrick J. Hearden points out that President Roosevelt's efforts to accommodate Jewish refugees fleeing from the Nazis were continually hampered by anti-Semitic sentiments in the United States, as well as the anti-immigration contingent in Congress.*

During the first eight years of the Great Depression, aliens likely to need public welfare were barred from entering the country. The State Department refused to issue visas to prospective immigrants unless they had enough money to support themselves without a job or unless they had friends or relatives in America who would provide for them. The vicious attack on Jews following the *Anschluss,* however, aroused humanitarian sentiment in the United States. President Roosevelt immediately decided to allow the maximum number of immigrants from Germany and Austria to come into the country under the provisions of the National Origins Quota Act. But widespread concern about unemployment, reinforced by grassroots nativism and anti-Semitism, kept Roosevelt from doing more to provide a haven for the oppressed in America. In fact, the State Department advised him that any effort to relax the immigration laws might backfire and provoke Congress to tighten existing regulations.

Patrick J. Hearden, *Roosevelt Confronts Hitler: America's Entry into World War II.* Dekalb: Northern Illinois University Press, 1987.

London) to the War Department in August 1944 to bomb Auschwitz. Much is made of John McCloy's response to Mr. Kubowitzki explaining the War Department's decision not to undertake such a mission. What is not on display and rarely mentioned is Leon Kubowitzki's July 1, 1944, letter to the executive director of the War Refugee Board arguing against bombing Auschwitz because "the first victims would be the Jews" and the Allied air assault would serve as "a welcome pretext for the Germans to assert that their Jewish victims have been massacred not by their killers, but by Allied bombers."

Informed Jewish opinion was against the whole idea of bombing Auschwitz. The very thought of the Allied forces deliberately killing Jews—to open the gates of Auschwitz so the survivors could run where?—was abhorrent then as it is now. The Rescue Committee of the Jewish Agency in Jerusalem voted against even making the bombing request—with Ben-Gurion the most outspoken opponent of all. Although only President Roosevelt or General Eisenhower could have ordered the bombing of Auschwitz, there is no record of any kind that indicates that either one was ever asked or even heard of the proposal—even though Jewish leaders of all persuasions had clear access to them both. . . .

If we had bombed Auschwitz with the inevitable consequence of killing hundreds, perhaps thousands of Jewish prisoners, I have no doubt that those who defame America for inaction would denounce us today for being accomplices in the Nazi genocide. Certainly Hitler and Goebbels would have justified their madness by claiming that the Allies, by their deliberate bombing of Auschwitz, had shown their own disdain for the value of Jewish lives.

The War Refugee Board

The War Refugee Board was created in January 1944, by President Roosevelt immediately upon presentation of the case for doing so by Henry Morgenthau. There were thousands of refugees stranded on the outer peripheries of Nazi Europe. With the invasion of Italy in 1943, thousands more sought safety in camps in the south. . . . Under pressure from Roosevelt and Churchill, Spain kept open its frontiers, stating as its policy that "all refugees without exception would be allowed to enter and remain." Probably more than 40,000 refugees, many of them Jewish, found safe sanctuary in Spain. . . .

Roosevelt's intervention with the government of Hungary, (which by then understood that Nazi defeat was inevitable), the actions of the War Refugee Board such as retaining Raoul Wallenberg in Budapest whose heroism we will always gratefully acknowledge, the bombing of the Budapest area—all played roles undoubtedly in the rescue of one-half of the Jewish community in Hungary. President Roosevelt was deeply and personally involved in the effort to save the Jews of Hungary. Listen to his statement to the nation on March 24, 1944:

> In one of the blackest crimes of all history—begun by the Nazis in the day of peace and multiplied by them a hundred times in time of war—the wholesale systematic murder of the Jews of Europe goes on unabated every hour. As a result of the events of the last few days hundreds of thousands of Jews who, while living under persecution, have at least found a haven from death in Hungary and the Balkans, are now threatened with annihilation as Hitler's forces descend more heavily upon these lands. That these innocent people, who have already survived a decade of Hitler's fury, should perish on the very eve of triumph over the barbarism which their persecution symbolizes, would be a major tragedy.

> It is therefore fitting that we should again proclaim our determination that none who participate in these acts of savagery shall go unpunished. The United Nations have made it clear that they will pursue the guilty and deliver them up in order that justice be done. That warning applies not only to the leaders but also to their functionaries and subordinates in Germany and in the

satellite countries. All who knowingly take part in the deportation of Jews to their death in Poland or Norwegians and French to their death in Germany are equally guilty with the executioner. All who share the guilt shall share the punishment.

In the meantime, and until the victory that is now assured is won, the United States will persevere in its efforts to rescue the victims of brutality of the Nazis and the Japs. In so far as the necessity of military operations permit this Government will use all means at its command to aid the escape of all intended victims of the Nazi and Jap executioner—regardless of race or religion or color. We call upon the free peoples of Europe and Asia temporarily to open their frontiers to all victims of oppression. We shall find havens of refuge for them, and we shall find the means for their maintenance and support until the tyrant is driven from their homelands and they may return. . . .

Nazi Responsibility

How ironic that our greatest president of this century—the man Hitler hated most, the leader constantly derided by the anti-Semites, vilified by [Nazi Propaganda Minister Joseph] Goebbels as a "mentally ill cripple" and as "that Jew Rosenfeld," violently attacked by the isolationist press—how ironic that he should be faulted for being indifferent to the genocide. For all of us, the shadow of doubt that enough was not done will always remain, even if there was little more that could have been done. But it is the killers who bear the responsibility for their deeds. To say that "we are all guilty" allows the truly guilty to avoid that responsibility. We must remember for all the days of our lives that it was Hitler who imagined the Holocaust and the Nazis who carried it out. We were not their accomplices. We destroyed them. . . .

Franklin Delano Roosevelt, more than any other American, is entitled to the historical credit for mobilizing and leading the forces that destroyed the Nazi barbarians and so saved western civilization. In the years of his leadership, he gave Jews dignity and self-respect as did no one before in American history. He understood and shared the anguish of the Holocaust as it unfolded.

Appendix of Documents

Document 1: Roosevelt Rallies the Nation

Following are excerpts from Franklin Roosevelt's first inaugural address, delivered on March 4, 1933, in which he inspired a nation crippled by the debilitating effects of the Great Depression to fight against the social and economic crisis.

I am certain that my fellow Americans expect that on my induction into the Presidency I will address them with a candor and a decision which the present situation of our Nation impels. This is preeminently the time to speak the truth, the whole truth, frankly and boldly. Nor need we shrink from honestly facing conditions in our country today. This great Nation will endure as it has endured, will revive and will prosper. So, first of all, let me assert my firm belief that the only thing we have to fear is fear itself—nameless, unreasoning, unjustified terror which paralyzes needed efforts to convert retreat into advance. In every dark hour of our national life a leadership of frankness and vigor has met with that understanding and support of the people themselves which is essential to victory. I am convinced that you will again give that support to leadership in these critical days. . . .

Our greatest primary task is to put people to work. This is no unsolvable problem if we face it wisely and courageously. It can be accomplished in part by direct recruiting by the Government itself, treating the task as we would treat the emergency of a war, but at the same time, through this employment, accomplishing greatly needed projects to stimulate and reorganize the use of our natural resources.

Hand in hand with this we must frankly recognize the over-balance of population in our industrial centers and, by engaging on a national scale in a redistribution, endeavor to provide a better use of the land for those best fitted for the land. . . .

In our progress toward a resumption of work we require two safeguards against a return of the evils of the old order: there must be a strict supervision of all banking and credits and investments, so that there will be an end to speculation with other people's money; and there must be provision for an adequate but sound currency.

These are the lines of attack. I shall presently urge upon a new Congress, in special session, detailed measures for their fulfillment, and I shall seek the immediate assistance of the several States. . . .

If I read the temper of our people correctly, we now realize as we have never realized before our interdependence on each other; that we cannot merely take but we must give as well; that if we are to go forward, we must move as a trained and loyal army willing to sacrifice for the good of a common discipline, because without such discipline no progress is made, no leadership becomes effective. We are, I know, ready and willing to submit our lives and property to such discipline, because it makes possible a leadership which aims at a larger good. This I propose to offer, pledging that the larger purposes will bind upon us all as a sacred obligation with a unity of duty hitherto evoked only in time of armed strife.

With this pledge taken, I assume unhesitatingly the leadership of this great army of our people dedicated to a disciplined attack upon our common problems. . . .

We do not distrust the future of essential democracy. The people of the United States have not failed. In their need they have registered a mandate that they want direct, vigorous action. They have asked for discipline and direction under leadership. They have made me the present instrument of their wishes. In the spirit of the gift I take it.

In this dedication of a Nation we humbly ask the blessing of God. May He protect each and every one of us. May He guide me in the days to come.

Franklin D. Roosevelt, first inaugural address, March 4, 1933, Washington, D.C.

Document 2: The Necessity of a Balanced Budget

On March 10, 1933, President Roosevelt sent a note to Congress pointing out the need for a balanced budget. In the following excerpts, Roosevelt explains that the recovery of the nation depends upon sound government credit.

For three long years the Federal Government has been on the road toward bankruptcy.

For the fiscal year 1931, the deficit was $462,000,000.

For the fiscal year 1932, it was $2,472,000,000.

For the fiscal year 1933, it will probably exceed $1,200,000,000.

For the fiscal year 1934, based on the appropriation bills passed by the last Congress and the estimated revenues, the deficit will probably exceed $1,000,000,000 unless immediate action is taken.

Thus we shall have piled up an accumulated deficit of $5,000,000,000.

With the utmost seriousness I point out to the Congress the profound effect of this fact upon our national economy. It has contributed to the recent collapse of our banking structure. It has accentuated the stagnation of the economic life of our people. It has added to the ranks of the unemployed. Our Government's house is not in order and for many reasons no effective action has been taken to restore it to order.

Upon the unimpaired credit of the United States Government rest the safety of deposits, the security of insurance policies, the activity of industrial enterprises, the value of our agricultural products and the availability of employment. The credit of the United States Government definitely affects those fundamental human values. It, therefore, becomes our first concern to make secure the foundation. National recovery depends upon it.

Franklin D. Roosevelt, "A Request to the Congress for Authority to Effect Drastic Economies in Government," March 10, 1933.

Document 3: Roosevelt's Lack of Direction

In the following excerpts from an article published in the August 1934 edition of Current History *magazine, noted journalist H.L. Mencken criticizes the lack of a clear sense of direction in the programs of the New Deal.*

Of late, I observe, the spokesmen for the Brain Trust have begun to abate their tall talk about planning, and to speak of experiment instead. Experiment it is—in a dingy and unclean laboratory, with cobwebs choking the microscopes, and every test-tube leaking. Such experiments are made by bulls in china shops, and by small boys turned loose in apple orchards. What, precisely, is the general idea underlying them in the present case? No one in Washington seems to know; and least of all the *Führer* [Roosevelt]. It remains, in fact, an unanswered question in the town whether he inclines toward the Left or toward the Right—which is to say, whether he is really for a Planned Economy or against it. One day the extreme revolutionaries seem to have the upper hand, and we are headed full tilt for communism, and the next day we beat a disorderly retreat to the Democratic platform of 1932. I dare say that most Americans would welcome any Planned Economy that showed the slightest sign of working, if only for the sake of getting rid of doubt and suspense, but how is the one we now hear of going to work so long as no two of its proponents agree as to where it is heading, or what it can accomplish, or what it is? How is it going to work so long as its devices are abandoned almost as fast as they are launched?

These questions the advocates of the New Deal appear to overlook. They are hot for it, but they neglect to explain why, save on grounds so general that it is impossible to make head or tail of them. In late weeks some of them have forsaken the defensive for the offensive. . . . Their contention, in brief, is that all the opponents of the Brain Trust are simply morons with a congenital antipathy to brains. Obviously, they have failed to notice that what causes the Brain Trust to be suspect is not the belief that it has brains but the rapid growth of an unhappy conviction that it lacks them. If it has them, then why are they not functioning? And if they are functioning, then why can't the brethren sit down together quietly, and come to some sort of agreement as to what they are driving at? One of their original promises, as connoisseurs will recall, was to put down that anthropophagous competition between man and man and class and class which, according to their theory, was to blame for all the sorrows of mankind. To what extent has this been accomplished? Only to the extent of subsidizing one class at the cost of another. The first class, by the Brain Trust premises, consisted wholly of virtuous innocents (mainly, it appears, farmers) who had suffered cruelly at the hands of the New Economy—but actually it included also the whole vast rabble of chronic mendicants and incurable unemployables. The second class, by the same premises, consisted wholly of speculators and exploiters—but actually it included also every American who had worked hard in the good times, and saved his money against a rainy day.

Quoted in William Dudley, ed., *The Great Depression: Opposing Viewpoints.* San Diego: Greenhaven Press, 1994, pp. 124–25.

Document 4: Defending Federal Work Relief

On May 6, 1939, Mrs. Florence Kerr, assistant administrator of the Works Progress Administration (WPA), addressed the closing session of the Regional Conference of Democratic Women of the Middle Western and Southwestern States in St. Louis, Missouri. In the following excerpts from that speech, Mrs. Kerr defends the WPA and other federal work relief programs championed by President Roosevelt.

There are some people today who disapprove of our Federal work program and would like to see it abolished, lock, stock and barrel. And there are more people who have heard so much bitter criticism of the WPA that they think maybe the critics are right. They wonder if maybe this "work relief business" is all a mistake.

It costs a lot of money. And it never seems to come to an end. It is true that we get a great deal for the money we spend on work relief. It is true that we get hundreds of thousands of miles of new and improved roads—thousands of schools, hospitals and other public buildings built or repaired—thousands of bridges—hundreds of new airports—thousands of parks, athletic fields, gymnasiums, swimming pools—thousands of miles of new water mains and sewers—hundreds of miles of levees—thousands of dams—millions of new trees planted in our state and national forests. But maybe it is all wrong—maybe we should get along without those roads and schools and hospitals and sewers and parks.

Our communities seem to approve of the work program—they ask for more and more WPA projects all the time and put up their own money to help pay for them. In the last three years our American communities have contributed over a billion dollars of their own to WPA projects for civic improvement. And the recent United States Community Appraisals, undertaken by the American Engineering Council and nine other independent national organizations, which report the views of nearly eight thousand county and town officials in communities large and small all over the United States, shows them overwhelmingly and almost unanimously in favor of the continuance of work relief. But maybe they don't know what they are talking about. Maybe the critics of the work program know better. Maybe it is a mistake to put our unemployed to work for the benefit of the communities in which they live. Maybe they should be maintained in enforced idleness on a starvation dole, losing their skills, losing their morale, losing all hope for themselves and all faith in American democracy.

Those who wish to destroy the Federal work program used to assure the American people that WPA workers were only a lot of bums and loafers—they didn't really work, they just leaned on their shovels. Tales about WPA shovel-leaners have had an immense circulation. But the publication of the inventory of accomplishments on WPA projects has sort of taken the humor out of those jokes. Two hundred and eighty thousand miles of roads and streets built and improved by the WPA—try to get a laugh out of that. Nearly three thousand new schoolhouses for our children, and over 21,000 repaired and modernized—what is there so funny about that? . . .

Our belief in the work program has had to undergo a great many trials. No human institution is perfect. The only question is whether our work program is something to be improved, or something to be destroyed. I think that it should be improved and I think that it is well worth defending as it stands, with all its human imperfections.

Florence Kerr, "America's Unfinished Business," available at www.newdeal.feri.org/works/wpa04.htm.

Document 5: "They Won't Work"

Following are excerpts from an article in the August 28, 1935, edition of the Nation, *in which the editors condemn the exaggerated portrayal of people who receive help from the government.*

Loose talk about the refusal of persons on relief to take jobs in private industry is growing rather than diminishing in volume. "They'd rather live on relief" has become a theme song among reactionaries, who find in it an argument perfectly suited to their purposes. A correspondent in California writes to tell us of an anonymous feature story which appeared in the *Los Angeles Times* of August 4 entitled "I Found Independence on the Dole." It purports to be a true story written by a woman who with her husband has been living on relief for several years. The author of the article boasts of numerous pleasure trips and other luxuries. "You see, during the past three or four years I've averaged $12 a week on my sewing and that's all for extras. I do not keep the cash in the house but send it by post-office money order to a friend back East who banks it for us." Once in a while, she says, she feels rather sorry for the woman who holds the mortgage on their property. "I try to be fair with her though. Last winter when she was ill and without funds I gave her $5.". . .

The viciousness of such propaganda is apparent. This particular story bears all the earmarks of having been manufactured. Yet the person of small means is in no mood to disbelieve it. It provides him with a scapegoat—the unemployed—on whom to blame his increasing misery. And it is easier to attack the poor devil clinging to the next lower rung of the ladder than to understand and combat the forces which are pushing both of them slowly downward.

Two weeks ago we adduced evidence to show the falseness of the charge that "they would rather live on relief." Since then Harry L. Hopkins, Federal Emergency Relief Administrator (FERA), has made public a study of alleged job refusals among relief clients in Washington which shows that out of 220 cases studied only 4 were found that could with justice be attributed to unwillingness to work. We have also received a copy of a bulletin issued in June by the FERA which contains the results of a similar investigation in Baltimore, Maryland, of 195 cases of alleged refusals. Here, too, the number of actual refusals was 4, while in a study made in Memphis, Tennessee, in 39 cases only one genuine refusal was found.

"They Won't Work," *Nation*, August 28, 1935.

Document 6: The New Deal and African Americans

This is an excerpt from an article written for the July 1935 edition of Opportunity, Journal of Negro Life *by Robert C. Weaver, an adviser on Negro affairs in the Department of the Interior. In the article, Weaver notes that in spite of many instances of abuse and discrimination, African Americans have benefited from New Deal programs.*

Although it is regrettable that the economic depression has led to the unemployment of so many Negroes and has threatened the creation of a large segment of the Negro population as a chronic relief load, one is forced to admit that Federal relief has been a godsend to the unemployed. The number of unemployed in this country was growing in 1933. According to the statistics of the American Federation of Labor, the number of unemployed increased from 3,216,000 in January, 1930 to 13,689,000 in March 1933. In November, 1934, the number was about 10,500,000 and although there are no comparable current data available, estimates indicate that current unemployment is less than that of last November. Local relief moneys were shrinking; and need and starvation were facing those unable to find an opportunity to work. A Federal relief program was the only possible aid in this situation. Insofar as the Negro was greatly victimized by the economic developments, he was in a position to benefit from a program which provided adequate funds for relief.

It is admitted that there were many abuses under the relief set-up. Such situations should be brought to light and fought. In the case of Negroes, these abuses undoubtedly existed and do exist. We should extend every effort to uncover and correct them. We can admit that we have gained from the relief program and still fight to receive greater and more equitable benefits from it.

Robert C. Weaver, "The Negro and the New Deal: A Look at the Facts," *Opportunity, Journal of Negro Life*, July 1935.

Document 7: "The Foundations of Our Democracy"

Following the introduction of President Roosevelt's plan to reorganize the Supreme Court, newspaper publisher Frank E. Gannett issued this statement expressing his concern that Roosevelt's idea of judicial reorganization was nothing more than a camouflaged attempt to broaden the powers of the executive branch of the government.

President Roosevelt has cleverly camouflaged a most amazing and startling proposal for packing the Supreme Court. It is true that the lower courts are slow and overburdened, we probably do need more judges to expedite litigation but this condition should not be used as a subtle excuse for changing the complexion and undermining the independence of our highest court. Increasing the number of judges from nine to fifteen would not make this high tribunal act any more promptly than it does now, but it would give the President control of the Judiciary Department.

A year ago I predicted that this is exactly what would happen if Roosevelt was reelected. The Supreme Court having declared invalid many of the administration measures, the President now resorts to a plan of creating a Supreme Court that will be entirely sympathetic with his ideas. Provision has been made for amending the Constitution. If it is necessary to change the Constitution it should be done in the regular way. The President is mistaken, if he thinks he can conceal his real purpose of packing, influencing and controlling the Supreme Court by confusing that objective with a long dissertation on the slow action of our various courts.

The Supreme Court has been the anchor that has held America safe through many storms. Its absolute independence and integrity must never be in doubt.

Our Government is composed of three departments, Legislative, Executive and Judiciary. These are the foundations of our Democracy. As a result of the election and the transfer of powers by so-called emergency measures, the Executive now dominates the Legislative Department. The President now proposes also to dominate the Judiciary. Do we want to give to this man or any one man complete control of these three departments of our Government which have from the beginning of the Republic been kept entirely separate and independent?

This proposal should give every American grave concern for it is a step towards absolutism and complete dictatorial power.

Statement by Frank E. Gannett, 1937. Available at www.nara.gov/education/teaching/conissues/separat.html

Document 8: Roosevelt Explains His Court Plan

Following are excerpts from President Roosevelt's fireside chat of March 9, 1937, in which he criticizes the Court for hampering his attempts to lead the nation out of the depression and describes his plan to reorganize the tribunal. Roosevelt also assures the American public that his plan would not result in a Court packed with "spineless puppets."

The American people have learned from the depression. For in the last three national elections an overwhelming majority of them voted a mandate that the Congress and the president begin the task of providing that protection—not after long years of debate, but now.

The courts, however, have cast doubts on the ability of the elected Congress to protect us against catastrophe by meeting squarely our modern social and economic conditions.

We are at a crisis, a crisis in our ability to proceed with that protection. It is a quiet crisis. There are no lines of depositors outside closed banks. But to the farsighted it is far-reaching in its possibilities of injury to America.

I want to talk with you very simply tonight about the need for present action in this crisis—the need to meet the unanswered challenge of one-third of a nation ill-nourished, ill-clad, ill-housed.

Last Thursday I described the American form of government as a three-horse team provided by the Constitution to the American people so that their field might be plowed. The three horses are, of course, the three branches of government—the Congress, the executive, and the courts. Two of the horses, the Congress and the executive, are pulling in unison today; the third is not. Those who have intimated that the president of the United States is trying to drive that team, overlook the simple fact that the president, as chief executive, is himself one of the three horses.

It is the American people themselves who are in the driver's seat.

It is the American people themselves who want the furrow plowed.

It is the American people themselves who expect the third horse to pull in unison with the other two. . . .

I want—as all Americans want—an independent judiciary as proposed by the framers of the Constitution. That means a Supreme Court that will enforce the Constitution as written, that will refuse to amend the Constitution by the arbitrary exercise of judicial power— in other words by judicial say-so. It does not mean a judiciary so independent that it can deny the existence of facts which are universally recognized. . . .

What is my proposal? It is simply this: whenever a judge or justice of any federal court has reached the age of seventy and does not avail himself of the opportunity to retire on a pension, a new member shall be appointed by the president then in office, with the approval, as required by the Constitution, of the Senate of the United States. . . .

Those opposing this plan have sought to arouse prejudice and fear by crying that I am seeking to "pack" the Supreme Court and that a baneful precedent will be established.

What do they mean by the words "packing the Supreme Court?"

Let me answer this question with a bluntness that will end all honest misunderstanding of my purposes.

If by that phrase "packing the Court" it is charged that I wish to place on the bench spineless puppets who would disregard the law and would decide specific cases as I wished them to be decided, I make this answer: that no president fit for his office would appoint, and no Senate of honorable men fit for their office would confirm, that kind of appointee to the Supreme Court.

But if by that phrase the charge is made that I would appoint and the Senate would confirm justices worthy to sit beside present members of the Court, who understand modern conditions, that I will appoint justices who will not undertake to override the judgment of the Congress on legislative policy, that I will appoint justices who will act as justices and not as legislators—if the appointment of such justices can be called "packing the Courts," then I say that I and with me the vast majority of the American people favor doing just that thing—now.

Franklin D. Roosevelt, "On the Reorganization of the Judiciary," available at www.newdeal.feri.org/chat09.htm.

Document 9: President Roosevelt Proclaims American Neutrality

The following excerpts are from Franklin Roosevelt's fireside chat of September 3, 1939. Following the outbreak of war in Europe, President Roosevelt assures the American public that the United States will remain neutral.

My countrymen and my friends. Tonight my single duty is to speak to the whole of America.

Until four-thirty o'clock this morning I had hoped against hope that some miracle would prevent a devastating war in Europe and bring to an end the invasion of Poland by Germany.

For four long years a succession of actual wars and constant crises have shaken the entire world and have threatened in each case to bring on the gigantic conflict which is today unhappily a fact.

It is right that I should recall to your minds the consistent and at times successful efforts of your government in these crises to throw the full weight of the United States into the cause of peace. In spite of spreading wars I think that we have every right and every reason to maintain as a national policy the fundamental moralities, the teachings of religion, the continuation of efforts to restore peace because some day, though the time may be distant, we can be of even greater help to a crippled humanity.

It is right, too, to point out that the unfortunate events of these recent years have, without question, been based on the use of force or the threat of force. And it seems to me clear, even at the outbreak of this great war, that the influence of America should be consistent in seeking for humanity a final peace which will eliminate, as far as it is possible to do so, the continued use of force between nations.

Let no man or woman thoughtlessly or falsely talk of America sending its armies to European fields. At this moment there is being prepared a proclamation of American neutrality. This would have been done even if there had been no neutrality statute on the books, for this proclamation is in accordance with international law and in accordance with American policy.

This will be followed by a proclamation required by the existing Neutrality Act. And I trust that in the days to come our neutrality can be made a true neutrality.

Franklin D. Roosevelt, "On the European War," September 3, 1939.

Document 10: A Promise with No Guarantee

In the following excerpt from his book After Seven Years, *former Roosevelt adviser Raymond Moley criticizes the president's approach to the war in Europe. Moley warns that Roosevelt's promise to aid the Allies and keep America from active participation in the war is a promise that cannot be kept.*

However well-intentioned this policy of building up support for our unneutral intervention in the affairs of Europe by arousing the fears and prejudices of the American people may be, the fact remains that it is a dangerous business. Hysteria rules by no half measures. When you touch off the powder of terror, you get not illumination but a blinding explosion. When you have awakened the animosities of a people, you have created the foreign policy that will carry you into war whether you will it or no. . . .

The promise implicit in all Roosevelt's moves—the promise in which he assuredly believes with all his heart—is that we can prevent or shorten war by active intervention in European affairs and still keep out of war ourselves. Unfortunately, it is a promise no living human being can guarantee. You cannot frankly give to one side in a quarrel what you withhold from the other side without courting, first, reprisals and, ultimately, hostilities. There is no such thing as a little unneutrality. When a nation declares and implements its hostile sentiments toward one side in a conflict, the chances that it can persuade that side of its disinterestedness are pretty slim. It is on this hairline margin of safety that we are now operating.

Raymond Moley, *After Seven Years*. Lincoln: University of Nebraska Press, 1939, pp. 383, 384.

Document 11: "Suppose My Neighbor's Home Catches Fire"

On December 17, 1940, President Roosevelt outlined the terms of the Lend-Lease program in a press conference. To put a human face on Great Britain's war situation Roosevelt compared the terms of Lend-Lease to a man lending his neighbor a hose to put out a fire.

Suppose my neighbor's home catches fire, and I have got a length of garden hose four or five hundred feet away; but, by Heaven, if he can take my garden hose and connect it up with his hydrant, I may help him to put out his fire. Now, what do I do? I don't say to him before that operation, "Neighbor, my garden hose cost me $15; you have got to pay me $15 for it:" What is the transaction that goes on? I don't want $15—I want my garden hose back after the fire is over. All right. If it goes through the fire all right, intact, without any damage to it, he gives it back to me and thanks me very much for the use of it. But suppose it gets smashed up—holes in it—during the fire; we don't have too much formality about it, but I say to him, "I was glad to lend you that hose; I see I can't use it any more, it's all smashed up." He says, "How many feet of it were there?" I tell him, "There were 150 feet of it." He says, "All right, I will replace it." Now, if I get a nice garden hose back, I am in pretty good shape. . . .

In other words, if you lend certain munitions and get the munitions back at the end of the war, if they are intact—haven't been hurt—you are all right; if they have been damaged or deteriorated or lost completely, it seems to me you come out pretty well if you have them replaced by the fellow that you have lent them to.

Quoted in Leonard Baker, *Roosevelt and Pearl Harbor*. New York: Macmillan, 1970, p. 75.

Document 12: Charles Lindbergh Speaks Out Against the War

World famous aviator Charles A. Lindbergh was a vocal critic of American intervention in World War II. The following excerpts are taken from a speech given at Madison Square Garden in New York on May 23, 1941. In the speech Lindbergh warns that democracy cannot be forced on the totalitarian regimes of Europe and Asia.

Our country is not divided today because we fear war, or sacrifice, or because we fear anything at all. We are divided because we are asked to fight over issues that are Europe's and not ours—issues that Europe created by her own short-sightedness. We are divided because many of us do not wish to fight again for England's balance of power, or for her domination of India, Mesopotamia, or Egypt, or for the Polish Corridor, or for another treaty like Versailles. We are divided because we do not want to cross an ocean to fight on foreign continents, for foreign causes, against an entire world combined against us. Many of us do not think we can impose our way of life, at the point of a machine gun, on the peoples of Germany, Russia, Italy, France, and Japan. Many of us do not believe democracy can be spread in such a manner. We believe that we are more likely to lose it at home than to spread it abroad by prolonging this war and sending millions of our soldiers to their deaths in Europe and Asia.

Democracy is not a quality that can be imposed by war. The attempt to do so has always met with failure. Democracy can spring only from within a nation itself, only from the hearts and minds of the people. It can be spread abroad by example, but never by force. The strength of a democracy lies in the satisfaction of its own people. Its influence lies in making others *wish* to copy it. If we cannot make other nations *wish* to copy our American system of government, we cannot force them to copy it by going to war.

Charles A. Lindbergh, *Autobiography of Values.* New York: Harcourt Brace Jovanovich, 1977, pp. 193–94.

Document 13: Executive Order 8802

On June 25, 1941, President Roosevelt signed Executive Order 8802. The Executive Order outlawed discrimination against African Americans in defense industries and created the Committee on Fair Employment Practice.

Whereas it is the policy of the United States to encourage full participation in the national defense program by all citizens of the United States, regardless of race, creed, color, or national origin, in the firm belief that the democratic way of life within the Nation can be defended successfully only with the help and support of all groups within its borders; and

Whereas there is evidence that available and needed workers have been barred from employment in industries engaged in defense production solely because of considerations of race, creed, color, or national origin, to the detriment of workers' morale and of national unity:

Now, therefore, by virtue of the authority vested in me by the Constitution and the statutes, and as a prerequisite to the successful conduct of our national defense production effort, I do hereby reaffirm the policy of the United States that there shall be no discrimination in the employment of workers in defense industries or government because of race, creed, color, or national origin, and I do hereby declare that it is the duty of employers and of labor organizations, in furtherance of said policy and of this order, to provide for the full and equitable participation of all workers in defense industries, without discrimination because of race, creed, color, or national origin;

And it is hereby ordered as follows:

1. All departments and agencies of the Government of the United States concerned with vocational and training programs for defense production shall take special measures appropriate to assure that such programs are administered without discrimination because of race, creed, color, or national origin;

2. All contracting agencies of the Government of the United States shall include in all defense contracts hereafter negotiated by them a provision obligating the contractor not to discriminate against any worker because of race, creed, color, or national origin;

3. There is established in the Office of Production Management a Committee on Fair Employment Practice, which shall consist of a chairman and four other members to be appointed by the President. The Chairman and members of the Committee shall serve as such without compensation but shall be entitled to actual and necessary transportation, subsistence and other expenses incidental to performance of their duties. The Committee shall receive and investigate complaints of discrimination in violation of the provisions of this order and shall take appropriate steps to redress grievances which it finds to be valid. The Committee shall also recommend to the several departments and agencies of the Government of the United States and to the President all measures which may be deemed by it necessary or proper to effectuate the provision of this order.

Franklin D. Roosevelt, Executive Order 8802, June 25, 1941.

Document 14: A Presidential Plea for Peace to the Emperor of Japan

Following are excerpts from a message sent by President Roosevelt to Japanese Emperor Hirohito on December 6, 1941—one day before the Japanese attack on Pearl Harbor. This personal appeal to the Japanese monarch was Roosevelt's final attempt to peacefully resolve tensions between the United States and Japan.

Only in situations of extraordinary importance to our two countries need I address Your Majesty messages on matters of state. I feel I should now so address you because of the deep and far-reaching emergency which appears to be in formation.

Developments are occurring in the Pacific area which threaten to deprive each of our nations and all humanity of the beneficial influence of the long peace between our two countries. Those developments contain tragic possibilities. . . .

More than a year ago Your Majesty's Government concluded an agreement with the Vichy Government by which five or six thousand Japanese troops were permitted to enter northern French Indochina for the protection of Japanese troops which were operating against China further north. And this Spring and Summer the Vichy Government permitted further Japanese military forces to enter into southern French Indochina for the common defense of French Indochina. I think I am correct in saying that no attack has been made upon Indochina nor that any has been contemplated.

During the past weeks it has become clear to the world that the Japanese military, naval, and air forces have been sent to southern Indochina in such large numbers as to create a reasonable doubt on the part of other nations that this continuing concentration in Indochina is not defensive in its character.

Because these continuing concentrations in Indochina have reached such large proportions and because they extend now to the southeast and the southwest corners of that peninsula it is only reasonable that the people of the Philippines, of the hundreds of islands of the East Indies, of Malaya, and of Thailand itself are asking themselves whether these forces of Japan are preparing or intending to make attack in one or more of these many directions.

I am sure that Your Majesty will understand that the fear of all these peoples is a legitimate fear inasmuch as it involves their peace and their national existence. I am sure that Your Majesty will understand why the people of the United States in such large numbers look askance at the establishment of military, naval and air bases manned and equipped so greatly as to constitute armed forces capable of measures of offense.

It is clear that a continuance of such a situation is unthinkable.

None of the people whom I have spoken of above can sit either indefinitely or permanently on a keg of dynamite.

There is absolutely no thought on the part of the United States of invading Indochina if every Japanese soldier or sailor were to be withdrawn therefrom.

I think that we can obtain the same assurance from the Governments of the East Indies, the Government of Malaya, and the Government of Thailand. I would even undertake to ask for the same assurance on the part of the Government of China. Thus a withdrawal of the Japanese forces from Indochina would result in the assurance of peace through the whole of the south Pacific area.

I address myself to Your Majesty so that Your Majesty may, as I am doing, give thought in this definite emergency to ways of dispelling the dark clouds. I am confident that both of us, for the sake of the peoples not only of our own great countries but for the sake of humanity in neighboring territories, have a sacred duty to restore traditional amity and prevent further death and destruction to the world.

Franklin D. Roosevelt, letter to Emperor Hirohito of Japan, December 6, 1941.

Document 15: "A Date Which Will Live in Infamy"

On December 7, 1941, the Japanese attacked the American Pacific Fleet at Pearl Harbor, Hawaii. In the following address, President Roosevelt asks Congress for a declaration of war against Japan.

Yesterday, December 7, 1941—a date which will live in infamy—the United States of America was suddenly and deliberately attacked by naval and air forces of the Empire of Japan.

The United States was at peace with that nation and, at the solicitation of Japan, was still in conversation with its Government and its Emperor looking toward the maintenance of peace in the Pacific. Indeed, one hour after Japanese air squadrons had commenced bombing in the American Island of Oahu, the Japanese Ambassador to the United States and his colleague delivered to our Secretary of State a formal reply to a recent American message. And while this reply stated that it seemed useless to continue the existing diplomatic negotiations, it contained no threat or hint of war or of armed attack.

It will be recorded that the distance of Hawaii from Japan makes it obvious that the attack was deliberately planned many days or even weeks ago. During the intervening time the Japanese Government has deliberately sought to deceive the United States by false statements and expressions of hope for continued peace.

The attack yesterday on the Hawaiian Islands has caused severe damage to American naval and military forces. I regret to tell you that very many American lives have been lost. In addition American ships have been reported torpedoed on the high seas between San Francisco and Honolulu.

Yesterday the Japanese Government also launched an attack against Malaya.

Last night Japanese forces attacked Hong Kong.
Last night Japanese forces attacked Guam.
Last night Japanese forces attacked the Philippine Islands.
Last night the Japanese attacked Wake Island.
And this morning the Japanese attacked Midway Island.

Japan has, therefore, undertaken a surprise offensive extending throughout the Pacific area. The facts of yesterday and today speak for themselves. The people of the United States have already formed their opinions and well understand the implications to the very life and safety of our nation.

As Commander-in-Chief of the Army and Navy I have directed that all measures be taken for our defense.

But always will our whole nation remember the character of the onslaught against us.

No matter how long it may take us to overcome this premeditated invasion, the American people in their righteous might will win through to absolute victory.

I believe that I interpret the will of the Congress and of the people when I assert that we will not only defend ourselves to the uttermost but will make it very certain that this form of treachery shall never again endanger us.

Hostilities exist. There is no blinking at the fact that our people, our territory and our interests are in grave danger.

With confidence in our armed forces—with the unbounding determination of our people—we will gain the inevitable triumph—so help us God.

I ask that the Congress declare that since the unprovoked and dastardly attack by Japan on Sunday, December seventh, 1941, a state of war has existed between the United States and the Japanese Empire.

Franklin D. Roosevelt, "War Message to Congress," December 8, 1941.

Document 16: The Japanese Threat

The following excerpts are taken from California attorney general Earl Warren's testimony given before the House Select Committee Investigating National Defense Migration on February 21 and 23, 1942. In his testimony, Warren argues that Japanese Americans living on the West Coast constitute a dangerous threat.

For some time I have been of the opinion that the solution of our alien enemy problem with all its ramifications, which include the descendants of aliens, is not only a Federal problem but is a military problem.

We believe that all of the decisions in that regard must be made by the military command that is charged with the security of this area. I am convinced that the fifth-column activities of our enemy call for the participation of people who are in fact American citizens, and that if we are to deal realistically with the problem we must realize that we will be obliged in time of stress to deal with subversive elements of our own citizenry.

If that be true, it creates almost an impossible situation for the civil authorities because the civil authorities cannot take protective measures against people of that character. We may suspect their loyalty. We may even have some evidence or, perhaps, substantial evidence of their disloyalty. But until we have the whole pattern of the enemy plan, until we are able to go into court and beyond the exclusion of a reasonable doubt establish the guilt of those elements among our American citizens, there is no way that civil government can cope with the situation.

On the other hand, we believe that in an area, such as in California, which has been designated as a combat zone, when things have happened such as have happened here on the coast, something should be done and done immediately. We believe that any delay in the adoption of the necessary protective measures is to invite disaster. It means that we, too, will have in California a Pearl Harbor incident.

I believe that up to the present and perhaps for a long time to come the greatest danger to continental United States is that from well organized sabotage and fifth-column activity. . . .

A wave of organized sabotage in California accompanied by an actual air raid or even by a prolonged black-out could not only be more destructive to life and property but could result in retarding the entire war effort of this Nation far more than the treacherous bombing of Pearl Harbor.

I hesitate to think what the result would be of the destruction of any of our big airplane factories in this State. It will interest you to know that some of our airplane factories in this State are entirely surrounded by Japanese land ownership or occupancy. It is a situation that is fraught with the greatest danger and under no circumstances should it ever be permitted to exist.

Quoted in William Dudley, ed., *World War II: Opposing Viewpoints.* San Diego: Greenhaven Press, 1997, pp. 200–201.

Document 17: Executive Order 9066

On February 19, 1942, President Roosevelt signed Executive Order 9066, authorizing the removal of Japanese Americans from sensitive military areas on the West Coast.

Whereas the successful prosecution of the war requires every possible protection against espionage and against sabotage to national-defense material, national-defense premises, and national-defense utilities as defined in section 4, Act of April 20, 1918, 40 Stat. 533, as amended by the Act of November 30, 1940, 54 Stat. 1220, and the Act of August 21, 1941, 55 Stat. 655 (U. S. C., Title 50, Sec. 104):

Now, therefore, by virtue of the authority vested in me as President of the United States, and Commander in Chief of the Army and Navy, I hereby authorize and direct the Secretary of War, and the Military Commanders whom he may from time to time designate, whenever he or any designated Commander deems such actions necessary or desirable, to prescribe military areas in such places and of such extent as he or the appropriate Military Commanders may determine, from which any or all persons may be excluded, and with such respect to which, the right of any person to enter, remain in, or leave shall be subject to whatever restrictions the Secretary of War or the appropriate Military Commander may impose in his discretion. The Secretary of War is hereby authorized to provide for residents of any such area who are excluded therefrom, such transportation, food, shelter, and other accommodations as may be necessary, in the judgement of the Secretary of War or the said Military Commander, and until other arrangements are made, to accomplish the purpose of this order. The designation of military areas in any region or locality shall supersede designations of prohibited and restricted areas by the Attorney General under the Proclamations of December 7 and 8, 1941, and shall supersede the responsibility and authority of the Attorney General under the said Proclamations in respect of such prohibited and restricted areas.

I hereby further authorize and direct the Secretary of War and the said Military Commanders to take such other steps as he or the appropriate Military Commander may deem advisable to enforce compliance with the restrictions applicable to each Military area hereinabove authorized to be designated, including the use of Federal troops and other Federal Agencies, with authority to accept assistance of state and local agencies.

I hereby further authorize and direct all Executive Departments, independent establishments and other Federal Agencies, to assist the Secretary of War or the said Military Commanders in carrying out this Executive Order, including the furnishing of medical aid, hospitalization, food, clothing, transportation, use of land, shelter, and other supplies, equipment, utilities, facilities and services.

This order shall not be construed as modifying or limiting in any way the authority heretofore granted under Executive Order No. 8972, dated December 12, 1941, nor shall it be construed as limiting or modifying the duty and responsibility of the Federal Bureau of Investigation, with respect to the investigation of alleged acts of sabotage or the duty and responsibility of the Attorney General and the Department of Justice under the Proclamations of December 7 and 8, 1941, prescribing regulations for the conduct and control of alien enemies, except as such duty and responsibility is superseded by the designation of military areas hereunder.

Franklin D. Roosevelt, Executive Order 9066, February 19, 1942. Available at www.dizzy.library. arizona.edu/images/jpamer/execordr.html.

CHRONOLOGY

JANUARY 30, 1882
Franklin Delano Roosevelt is born in Hyde Park, New York.

MARCH 17, 1905
Roosevelt marries Eleanor Roosevelt, niece to his distant cousin President Theodore Roosevelt.

NOVEMBER 8, 1910
Roosevelt is elected state senator from New York's twenty-sixth district.

MARCH 1913
Roosevelt is appointed assistant secretary of the Navy by President Woodrow Wilson.

AUGUST 1914
World War I begins in Europe.

APRIL 6, 1917
Congress, at the request of President Wilson, declares war on Germany.

JUNE 28, 1919
The Treaty of Versailles brings World War I to an end.

NOVEMBER 19, 1919
The Senate rejects the Treaty of Versailles.

AUGUST 10, 1921
Roosevelt contracts polio.

NOVEMBER 6, 1928
Roosevelt is elected governor of New York.

OCTOBER 1929
The Stock Market crashes on Wall Street. The Great Depression begins.

December 1930

The Hoover administration announces that 4.5 million Americans are out of work; The large and once-powerful Bank of the United States fails; Roosevelt declares President Hoover's anti-depression measures to be too radical and too costly.

1932–1936

A four-year drought creates the "Dust Bowl" from Texas to the Dakotas.

April 1932

The "Brains Trust" is organized to advise presidential candidate Roosevelt on the key issues for the 1932 election.

November 8, 1932

Franklin D. Roosevelt, promising a "New Deal" to help Americans suffering from the effects of the Great Depression, crushes Herbert Hoover in the presidential election.

December 1932

Unemployment reaches nearly 13 million.

January 30, 1933

Adolf Hitler is named chancellor of Germany.

March 4, 1933

Franklin D. Roosevelt is inaugurated the thirty-second president of the United States.

March 6, 1933

Roosevelt shuts down the American banking system by declaring a bank holiday.

March 9, 1933

The Seventy-third Congress convenes. That same evening it passes the Emergency Banking Act.

March 10, 1933

Roosevelt delivers a special message to Congress calling for spending cuts to eliminate a $5 billion deficit.

MARCH 12, 1933
Roosevelt gives his first "fireside chat" to assure the American people of the safety of bank deposits.

MARCH 31, 1933
The Civilian Conservation Corps is established.

MAY 12, 1933
The Federal Emergency Relief Act is passed, setting up the first national system of relief programs; The Agricultural Adjustment Act creates a national plan for agriculture through a system that pays farmers to take land out of cultivation.

MAY 18, 1933
The Tennessee Valley Authority Act provides for federal funding for the development of the Tennessee Valley.

JUNE 16, 1933
The National Industrial Recovery Act provides for a system of industrial codes and for a $3.3 billion public works program; The Glass-Steagall Act divorces commercial from investment banking and guarantees bank deposits.

JANUARY 1934
The Civil Works Administration under the leadership of Harry Hopkins reaches its peak as it employs 4,230,000 people.

MAY 1935
The Supreme Court declares the National Industrial Recovery Act unconstitutional.

AUGUST 1935
Roosevelt signs the Social Security Act providing workers with retirement annuities financed by taxes on their wages and on their employers payroll.

FEBRUARY 1936
The Supreme Court declares the Agricultural Adjustment Act unconstitutional.

MARCH 7, 1936

Germany reoccupies the Rhineland in open defiance of the Treaty of Versailles.

NOVEMBER 1936

Roosevelt is reelected, soundly defeating Republican candidate Governor Alf Landon of Kansas.

FEBRUARY 1937

Roosevelt sends Congress his plan for reorganizing the Supreme Court by adding a new justice (up to a maximum of six) for each sitting justice who refuses to retire at age seventy.

APRIL 1937

The Supreme Court invalidates a New York state minimum wage law.

MAY 1937

The Supreme Court upholds the constitutionality of the Social Security Act.

JULY 1937

Congress kills the Roosevelt "court packing" scheme.

NOVEMBER 9, 1938

A massive, coordinated attack on Jews throughout Nazi Germany becomes known as *Kristallnacht* or "The Night of the Broken Glass."

NOVEMBER 15, 1938

Roosevelt condemns Nazi anti-Semitism and recalls the American ambassador to Germany.

MAY 10, 1939

Winston Churchill becomes prime minister of Great Britain.

MAY 27, 1939

The *St. Louis*, a ship carrying nearly 1,000 Jewish refugees fleeing from the Nazis, arrives in Havana, Cuba. All but twenty-two are refused entry into Cuba or the United States and are sent back to Europe to face the Nazis.

SEPTEMBER 1, 1939
Germany invades Poland.

SEPTEMBER 3, 1939
Great Britain and France declare war on Germany.

SEPTEMBER 5, 1939
Roosevelt officially proclaims America neutral.

NOVEMBER 4, 1939
Roosevelt signs the Neutrality Act of 1939, which revises American neutrality laws to permit Germany's enemies to buy American goods on a "cash and carry" basis.

JUNE 22, 1940
France surrenders to Germany. England stands alone against Nazi-dominated Europe.

AUGUST 8–OCTOBER 31, 1940
The Battle of Britain rages in the skies over England. The German Luftwaffe fails to destroy the Royal Air Force and secure the skies for a German invasion.

SEPTEMBER 3, 1940
Great Britain and the United States announce the "destroyers-for-bases" deal, in which the United States lends Great Britain fifty destroyers in exchange for the right to construct U.S. military bases on British possessions in the Western Hemisphere.

SEPTEMBER 27, 1940
Japan signs the Tripartite Agreement with Germany and Italy.

OCTOBER 30, 1940
Roosevelt, campaigning for an unprecedented third term, tells American parents that "your boys aren't going to be sent into any foreign wars."

NOVEMBER 2, 1940
Roosevelt defeats Republican Wendell Wilkie in the presidential election.

MARCH 11, 1941

Congress passes the Lend-Lease Act, authorizing Roosevelt to turn America into an "arsenal of democracy" for Great Britain and other countries fighting Nazi aggression.

JUNE 22, 1941

Germany invades the Soviet Union; Roosevelt promises aid to the Soviets.

JUNE 25, 1941

Roosevelt signs Executive Order 8802 banning discrimination in employment in defense industries and creating the Fair Employment Practices Commission to enforce the ban.

JULY 25, 1941

Responding to Japan's military occupation of the French colony of Indochina, Roosevelt freezes all Japanese assets in the United States and places General Douglas MacArthur in charge of defending the Philippines.

SEPTEMBER 11, 1941

Roosevelt delivers his "shoot on sight" address announcing that navy ships are to aggressively defend themselves against attacks by Axis ships and submarines.

OCTOBER 31, 1941

The *Reuben James,* an American destroyer patrolling the Atlantic, becomes the first armed American ship to be destroyed by a German submarine.

NOVEMBER 1941

Talks between the United States and Japan break down as the two sides reject each other's peace proposals.

DECEMBER 7, 1941

The Japanese attack the American Pacific Fleet at Pearl Harbor, Hawaii, and launch offensives against the Philippines and Hong Kong.

DECEMBER 8, 1941

Congress declares war on Japan.

December 11, 1941
Germany and Italy declare war on the United States.

January 2, 1942
The Philippines fall to the Japanese.

February 19, 1942
Roosevelt signs Executive Order 9066 authorizing the military evacuation and internment of 120,000 Japanese Americans from the West Coast.

November 8, 1942
Allied troops under General Dwight D. Eisenhower land in North Africa.

July 10, 1943
Allied armies invade Sicily.

July 24–25, 1943
Italian dictator Benito Mussolini is overthrown and imprisoned.

September 8, 1943
Italy surrenders to the Allies.

September 10, 1943
German troops seize Rome.

January 26, 1944
Roosevelt creates the War Refugee Board.

June 6, 1944
Allied forces launch the D-Day invasion of Normandy, France.

August 10, 1944
American forces capture Guam.

August 25, 1944
Allied armies liberate Paris.

November 7, 1944
Roosevelt is elected to a fourth term.

December 16, 1944

Hitler launches the Battle of the Bulge, the last German offensive of the war.

January 20, 1945

Nearly all Japanese Americans in relocation centers are permitted to leave.

April 1945

Allied forces liberate Nazi concentration camps at Buchenwald, Dachau, and Bergen-Belsen.

April 12, 1945

Roosevelt dies at Warm Springs, Georgia; Vice President Harry S. Truman becomes president.

April 30, 1945

Adolf Hitler commits suicide.

May 2, 1945

Berlin falls to Soviet forces.

May 7, 1945

Germany surrenders to the Allies.

August 6, 1945

The United States drops an atomic bomb on Hiroshima, Japan.

August 9, 1945

The United States drops a second atomic bomb on Nagasaki, Japan.

September 2, 1945

World War II is officially brought to an end when Japanese sign final surrender terms aboard the American battleship *Missouri*.

FOR FURTHER RESEARCH

THE DEPRESSION AND THE NEW DEAL

BERNARD BELLUSH, *The Failure of the NRA*. New York: Norton, 1975.

RUSSELL D. BUHITE AND DAVID W. LEVY, eds., *FDR's Fireside Chats*. Norman: University of Oklahoma Press, 1992.

JAMES M. BURNS, *Roosevelt: The Lion and the Fox*. New York: Harcourt Brace, 1956.

JOHN FRANKLIN CARTER, *The New Dealers, by Unofficial Observer*. New York: Simon and Schuster, 1934.

PAUL K. CONKIN, *The New Deal*. New York: Thomas Crowell, 1967.

KENNETH DAVIS, *FDR: The New Deal Years, 1933–1937*. New York: Random House, 1986.

THOMAS H. ELIOT, *Recollections of the New Deal: When the People Mattered*. Boston: Northeastern University Press, 1992.

JOHN T. FLYNN, *The Roosevelt Myth*. New York: Devon-Adair, 1956.

FRANK FREIDEL, *F.D.R. and the South*. Baton Rouge: Louisiana State University Press, 1965.

JOHN B. KIRBY, *Black Americans in the Roosevelt Era: Liberalism and Race*. Knoxville: University of Tennessee Press, 1980.

WILLIAM E. LEUCHTENBURG, *Franklin D. Roosevelt and the New Deal, 1932–1940*. New York: Harper and Row, 1963.

WILLIAM E. LEUCHTENBURG, ed., *The Supreme Court Reborn: The Constitutional Revolution in the Age of Roosevelt*. New York: Oxford University Press, 1995.

ROBERT MCELVAINE, ed., *The Great Depression: America, 1929–1941*. New York: Random House, 1985.

BROADUS MITCHELL, *Depression Decade*. New York: Rinehart, 1947.

RAYMOND MOLEY, *After Seven Years.* Lincoln: University of Nebraska Press, 1971.

DON NARDO, ed., *Turning Points in World History: The Great Depression.* San Diego: Greenhaven Press, 2000.

BASIL RAUCH, *The History of the New Deal, 1933–1938.* New York: Octagon Books, 1975.

EDGAR EUGENE ROBINSON, *The Roosevelt Leadership, 1933–1945.* Philadelphia: J.B. Lippincott, 1955.

ELIOT A. ROSEN, *Hoover, Roosevelt, and the Brains Trust: From Depression to New Deal.* New York: Columbia University Press, 1977.

SAMUEL I. ROSENMAN, ed., *The Public Papers and Addresses of Franklin D. Roosevelt.* 13 vols. New York: Russell and Russell, 1969.

ARTHUR M. SCHLESINGER JR., *The Coming of the New Deal.* Boston: Houghton Mifflin, 1959.

HARVARD SITKOFF, *A New Deal for Blacks.* New York: Oxford University Press, 1978.

STUDS TERKEL, *Hard Times: An Oral History of the Great Depression.* New York: Random House, 1970.

CHARLES TROUT, *The Great Depression and the New Deal.* New York: Oxford University Press, 1977.

REXFORD G. TUGWELL, *The Brains Trust.* New York: Viking Press, 1968.

———, *The Democratic Roosevelt.* Garden City, NY: Doubleday, 1957.

GEORGE WOLFSKILL, *Revolt of the Conservatives.* Indianapolis: Bobbs-Merrill, 1966.

WORLD WAR II

LEONARD BAKER, *Roosevelt and Pearl Harbor.* New York: Macmillan, 1970.

CHARLES A. BEARD, *President Roosevelt and the Coming of War, 1941.* New Haven, CT: Yale University Press, 1948.

Wayne S. Cole, *Roosevelt and the Isolationists, 1932–1945.* Lincoln: University of Nebraska Press, 1983.

Robert Dallek, *Franklin D. Roosevelt and American Foreign Policy, 1932–1945.* New York: Oxford University Press, 1981.

Roger Daniels, *Prisoners Without Trial: Japanese-Americans in World War II.* New York: Hill and Wang, 1993.

Roger Daniels, ed., *American Concentration Camps: A Documentary History of the Relocation and Incarceration of Japanese-Americans, 1942–1945.* New York: Garland Press, 1989.

Kenneth S. Davis, *FDR: Into the Storm, 1937–1940.* New York: Random House, 1993.

Robert Divine, ed., *Causes and Consequences of World War II.* Chicago: Quadrangle, 1969.

John Dower, *War Without Mercy: Race and Power in the Pacific War.* New York: Pantheon Books, 1986.

William Dudley, ed., *World War II: Opposing Viewpoints.* San Diego: Greenhaven Press, 1997.

Thomas R. Fehrenbach, *FDR's Undeclared War, 1939–1941.* New York: David McKay, 1967.

Frank Freidel, *Franklin D. Roosevelt: A Rendezvous with Destiny.* Boston: Little, Brown, 1990.

Walter Johnson, *The Battle Against Isolation.* New York: Da Capo Press, 1973.

Gabriel Kolko, *The Politics of War, 1943–1945.* New York: Random House, 1968.

Joseph P. Lash, *Roosevelt and Churchill, 1939–1941: The Partnership That Saved the West.* New York: Norton, 1976.

Arthur D. Morse, *While Six Million Died: A Chronicle of American Apathy.* New York: Ace, 1967.

Gordon W. Prange, *At Dawn We Slept: The Untold Story of Pearl Harbor.* New York: McGraw-Hill, 1981.

Paul Schroeder, *The Axis Alliance and Japanese-American Relations, 1941.* Ithaca, NY: Cornell University Press, 1958.

A.J.P. TAYLOR, *The Origins of the Second World War*. New York: Atheneum, 1961.

STUDS TERKEL, *"The Good War": An Oral History of World War II*. New York: Pantheon, 1984.

JOHN TOLAND, *Infamy: Pearl Harbor and Its Aftermath*. Garden City, NY: Doubleday, 1982.

JONATHAN G. UTLEY, *Going to War with Japan, 1937–1941*. Knoxville: University of Tennessee Press, 1985.

ROBERTA WOHLSLETTER, *Pearl Harbor: Warning and Decision*. Stanford, CA: Stanford University Press, 1962.

DAVID S. WYMAN, *The Abandonment of the Jews: America and the Holocaust, 1941–1945*. New York: Pantheon, 1984.

INDEX

achievements of, 69

agricultural program of, 49, 73, 86

aid to blacks, 169

business proposals of, 73–74

and civil rights, 169–73

criticism of, 67–68, 87, 92
  as break with tradition, 88–89
  FDR on, 55

historical evaluations of, 30–31

humanitarianism of, 92–93

marked beginning of the welfare state, 61–71

never endangered free enterprise system, 91

New Republic, 87

New York Times, 132

Niblack (destroyer) incident, 140
  Hitler's reaction to, 142–43

Nixon, Richard, 59

Nomura, Kichisaburo, 158, 162, 187

Norris, George, 115

Norris-LaGuardia Act, 53–54

O'Donnell, John, 141

O'Neill, William L., 39

Open Door policy, 150

Panama Conference, 138

Pearl Harbor, 165

Perkins, Frances, 21–22, 56

Personal Justice Denied (Commission on Wartime Relocation and Internment of Civilians), 42

Pittman, Key, 101

Plessy v. Ferguson, 171

Polk, James K., 151

Powell, Adam Clayton, Jr., 172

Prange, Gordon W., 158

President's Committee on Fair Employment Practices, 172

public opinion
  on support of U.S. going to war, 35, 150–51

Public Works Administration (PWA), 28–29, 64

Raeder, Erich, 138, 143

Randolph, A. Philip, 172

Reconstruction Finance Corporation, 25

Reed, Stanley, 98, 108

refugees, Jewish, 39
  currency restrictions on, 200–201
  Evian Conference on, 206
  FDR did not do enough for, 195–203
  con, 204–16
  as percent of U.S. immigration, 208

Rehnquist, William H., 174

Reilly, Mike, 14

Republicans
  support of New Deal policies by, 58–59

Reuben James (destroyer) attack, 37, 145–46

Richberg, Donald, 103

Roberts, Owen, 98, 101, 104
  shift in opinions of, 105

Robeson, Paul, 171

Robin Moor (merchant ship) sinking, 143

Robinson, Joseph T., 101,